*Silhouettes*

# SILHOUETTES

## Women
## behind
## Great
## Men

*by*
*Helen Kooiman*

WORD BOOKS, PUBLISHER
Waco, Texas

DEDICATED *to the women of the world*

*who need to be reminded of what it is*

*that produces true greatness in a man*

# Contents

# Acknowledgments

Shortly after the book *Cameos: Women Fashioned by God* was published, I received a phone call from a friend who suggested the idea and title for this book, *Silhouettes: Women behind Great Men*. I am indebted to Freeman Lawrence for that call!

And I am deeply grateful to each individual about whom I have written—these women of God and the men in their lives. Many of the men traveled hundreds of miles, some thousands, to meet me at the homes of their mothers in order to assist in the telling of the stories. For opening their homes and hearts to me, I have no words to adequately express my appreciation.

I wish also to acknowledge the special help received from the following people: Elton Whisenhunt, Director of Public Relations for the Wallace E. Johnson Enterprises; Mrs. Florence Skinner and Mrs. Clarence Gray, sisters of Dr. Bill Bright; Mrs. Edith Guthrie, sister of Dr. W. A. Criswell; the many individuals at Calvary Baptist Church and the Hotel Salisbury in New York City who provided cozy accommodations and extended their warm friendship; Dave and Darlene Swanson; Mr. and Mrs. Howard Thompson, and Dr. and Mrs. Grant Thompson in Canada; Melvin Graham, and Mrs. Leighton Ford and Mrs. S. J. McElroy, sisters of Billy Graham; Mr. and Mrs. James Rough, hosts to the Mata'afas from Samoa; Sara LeTourneau, sister of R. G. LeTourneau, and Flora Barclay, Sara's companion; Paul Smith, brother of "Chuck" Smith, and Virginia Fromm, sister of "Chuck" Smith.

Thanks to H. Edward Rowe, President of Christian Freedom Foundation, for his encouragement and understanding; and to Rowena Boehne, Judy Robles, and Audrey Juroe who assisted in typing. Thanks to Val Hellikson, President of the "Haven of Rest" and to Dr. Lowell Saunders for prayer support and help.

To many others known and unknown by name who have shared in this undertaking by providing help and information and supportive prayer, my thanks.

Two friends followed every page of this writing and the traveling involved with great concern—Marj Chartrand and Thelma Elfstrom: thank you for what you have done for me, and what you mean to me!

And last, but not least, a special "mother's thanks" to three very special children—Tonia, Rhonda, and Kraig—without your love, patience, and cooperation this book would only have been a dream and a prayer.

# Introduction

Many women achieve distinction and reach great heights in life through notable contributions, some in the arts, others as teachers or leaders in some other professions. Then there are those, like the silhouettes in this book, whose attainments would not make them likely candidates for fame or recognition; yet, they may be mothers of great sons or daughters or be wives of great men.

The men whom we are referring to as "great" would be the first to disclaim any greatness. It is our human tendency to ascribe the term "great" to those who have achieved or contributed in some special way to the world in which we live. This book concerns itself with men of this stature and the women behind them.

The Bible cautions against attaching undue emphasis and importance to a person's position in life (see for example Matthew 22:16; Acts 10:34; and James 2:1–9). This is the firm conviction of the individuals included within this volume as well as my own.

It has not been my intention to make these women appear as plaster saints. While it is true that their virtues have been shown, they would tell you they are not perfect. These special women, about whom an aura of genuineness exists, reveal great spiritual resources and Christian graces.

The beauty of these women has given me an understanding of what it is that has produced and contributed to the greatness of the men they are behind. If the women had been anything less, quite possibly the men in their lives would not be what they are. Many men have succeeded in spite of the women in their lives; yet it is undeniably true that a mother and wife can be a great influence that spurs a man on to achievement and greatness. I agree with Taylor Caldwell who said: "The decay and ruin of a nation has always been at the hands of its women. So does its life and strength, its reverence for beauty, its mercy and kindness, and above all—its men."

11

Meeting these men and the women behind them has resulted in some of the choicest, most beautiful, and enriching experiences of my life. I treasure the memory of each visit and the love and warmth that was shown and expressed. I trust that I have conveyed within these pages that which I have experienced so that you, likewise, may be helped and encouraged.

In the Bible, Hebrews 11, we have what is often called "The Roll Call of Faith" chapter. Here we are introduced to "Men of God [who] in days of old were famous for their faith" (v. 2, *The Living Bible*). If the men and women mentioned in this book are to be remembered for anything, let it be for their faith as contemporary Christians.

# Bessie Santmire Olford

### mother of STEPHEN F. OLFORD

It was Sunday in Portuguese West Africa. Sunday was always a special day but made more so this particular time because it was a little boy's seventh birthday with presents, cake, and candles—even on the mission field. The father of the home, Frederick Olford, turned to his wife and said, "Mother, this has been such a wonderful day. I think you should take the devotions tonight."

Bessie Olford smiled knowingly at her husband. It had been prearranged. "Boys, tonight I'm going to read about the Lord's return." And she opened the well-worn family Bible and read, "I will come again, and receive you unto myself; that where I am, there ye may be also" (John 14:3). She paused, looked at her older son and said, "Stephen, when the Lord Jesus comes back, will you be ready to meet him?"

Being a very wise mother, she didn't press the question but went on to add, "You know, your friends will go. Your brother John will go. Daddy and Mother will go. Will you go?" Seven-year-old Stephen, the birthday-boy, fidgeted nervously with his fingers. He wished that she wouldn't look so directly at him. He wanted to crawl under the dinner table—anything to get away. He dropped his eyes so as not to meet her concerned, penetrating gaze. When she ended the family devotional period with prayer, Stephen Olford listened carefully. He thought to himself: Will I go?

Then it was bedtime. From darkness to dawn wild animals could be heard prowling about outside. Sometimes they even ventured very near the house, and the Olford boys were glad for the snug safety of their beds and the knowledge that their mother and father were nearby.

Stephen fell into a restless sleep. For hours he tossed and turned. He tried thinking out all of his plans for the next day, but they vanished in the overwhelming consciousness of his unreadiness to meet Jesus. Suddenly the thought struck him: Suppose he has come already? A fear gripped his soul, and cupping his hands around his mouth he called out into the darkness, "Mother! Mother!" There was no reply.

Stephen called out again. "Mother! Mother!!" There was still no answering response. Now he was really frightened. He sat upright and this time screamed out, "MOTHER!" and to his utter relief she came rushing in.

"Stephen, Stephen, what's the matter? Is there a hyena outside? Is there some animal pawing at your window?" As she stood by his side, drawing him close against her, she felt his little body tremble.

"Oh no, Mother, it was much worse than that. I thought Jesus had come, and I had been left behind." She drew him even closer, murmuring comforting words of understanding. Then she lit the lamp, found her Bible, opened it, and read to him what has since become one of Stephen Olford's favorite verses, Colossians 1:27. The last part of that verse says, "Christ in you, the hope of glory."

Taking his little hands in hers she said: "If you want to be sure of going to heaven, Stephen, then you must have Christ in you—in your heart."

"Stephen," she said, "do you want to invite Jesus into your

heart?" He nodded, and together mother and son knelt by the bed-side.

Of that evening Stephen Olford says, "Before, my pillow seemed stuffed with bricks, but now a wonderful peace came into my heart. Mother was the undergirding of that conversion. In those early formative years it was her training, her teaching, her example and counseling that drew me to the Lord."

Bessie Olford would never dodge an issue. Dr. Olford has de-scribed her as being "like quicksilver," ever alert to what was going on about her. "When I was worried about something," he explains, "she would say, 'Now, Stephen, what's troubling you? Let's sit down and talk it over.' " And they would. Hers were the ways of wisdom.

Bessie Santmire was born in Buffalo, New York, on January 22, 1893. Sorrow came early into her life. As a child of seven she was bereft of her mother and was taken into the home of her married sister in nearby Blasdell. Of her experience in coming to know Christ she says: "I was saved after a talk with my sister, when I was nine years of age."

Many friendships were formed in Blasdell which were later to prove of great value. She was brought into the life of a small, but active Sunday school.

To test her fortitudes it was decided that a time away from home would further strengthen the spiritual and physical life of this far from robust young woman; so early in 1914 Bessie was a student at Toronto Bible College.

She heard of the need for missionaries in Central Africa. The Lord spoke to the heart of young twenty-year-old Bessie, and she made the decision to go to the mission field.

It seemed advisable for her to travel to Africa with Mr. and Mrs. Leonard Gammon, who were returning to the field. Their destina-tion was the station of Luma-Casai, where they were met by Mr. and Mrs. Cuthbert Taylor and Frederick Olford. Mr. Olford had seen her photograph and had the feeling that they were to become more than friends and co-workers.

Frederick Olford was a Britisher through and through, born in Devonport, Devonshire. After receiving Bible and medical training he went to the mission station in Angola where, as the ways of love would have it, he was to meet the sweet-faced young woman whose photograph he had admired.

Courtship for the two missionaries was difficult. Even though they were on the same mission station, they had to write notes and pass them to one another in hymnbooks. Only now and again, under tremendous shielding, could they hold hands or converse.

One day a dog came up behind Bessie and pushed her over. As she fell she dislocated her kneecap. Mr. Olford had to be called. His minor medical training made him the only person qualified on the mission station to put her knee back into place. "He made a crutch for me, and it was then that I thought him really wonderful!"

Two years after arriving at Luma-Casai, Bessie and Frederick were married. "Though we had never been out together, or spent an evening alone until after our wedding, we knew God had brought us together."

Bessie Santmire was an answer to Frederick's prayer. At the age of twenty-one he arrived on the mission field. After mastering the difficult tongue, it troubled young Frederick that his evangelical zeal wasn't getting across to the people. Finally it became a real issue, and he faced one of the chiefs and said, "Why don't you respond to the gospel?"

The chief looked at the young white missionary and answered, "When you become married, and when you bring up children and can demonstrate to us that your religion works in a family unit, then I will believe it, and my people will begin to believe it."

Dr. Stephen F. Olford tells of his birth, as it was related to him, in this manner: "My father took very seriously the words of the African chief. I was the first child born to them, and they tell me that my parents traveled three weeks into British territory to secure the help of a doctor. Mother was transported in a hammock by native carriers, but father walked every mile of the way!

"A few weeks after my birth, they started the long journey back. I was carried on the top of the head of an African boy in a little carrycot. On several occasions during this exacting journey I was exposed to many kinds of dangers and perils. At one juncture, the African carrying me had to wade through a flooding river infested with crocodiles. Every step he took might well have been the last!"

What a reception from the natives awaited the Olfords when the journey back to the mission village had been completed. Now the white man was really "one of them." Dr. Olford explains that reception like this: "Mother and Father would take this little bundle of life and hand me out to the chief, and from the chief I would be handed to the underlings right around to all the villagers. I have heard my father speak in missionary gatherings, as giving me out as

16

life and getting me back as life abundant—full of lice and what not!"

The work of the Lord prospered as it had never prospered before. This was a symbol of peace, of goodwill. The former resistance of the village chief was broken down. And with the breakdown of his resistance came the much-longed-for movement of the Holy Spirit. Now the work could proceed with strong evangelistic zeal.

Mrs. Olford loved celebrations. Every opportunity was used for a happy time. Christmas in Africa arrived in the middle of what was their summer season. The Olford home was the gathering place for all the other missionaries. Decorations went up with the children joining in the merriment of the occasion. She greatly enjoyed providing happiness for others. Her son says, "She was terrifically hospitable, the house was always neat, everything was in place—and yet, not in that fussy way that puts everyone ill at ease."

Her thoughtfulness spilled over into remembering people on their birthdays, but she was just as good at sharing the days of sorrow and the times of sickness. When someone lost a loved one, Mrs. Olford would make a note of this, and a year later would send that person a special note of condolence, or, if possible, she would call them or make a personal visit. It showed a heart in tune with divine love.

As a boy, Stephen accompanied his father on treks to the tribesmen. There he saw witchcraft, idolatry, and superstition in action. On one occasion he sat with his father around a campfire and watched as the tribesmen plucked meat from human bones. These were dangerous trips, but the dynamic faith of Bessie Olford rested serenely in the mercy and will of her all-knowing heavenly Father.

Mrs. Olford knew what it was to awaken in the morning and hear her offspring squeal out, "Oh, there's a snake in my boot!" She knew what it was to have a leopard leap through the window and devour one of their pet dogs. Justifiable fear was her portion, too, as her son became lost in a native village for many hours. She saw her son hurled through the air as he was being carried across a fast flowing stream, landed on a tree branch which caught and held him. Danger was no stranger. And neither was God's providential care!

Bessie Olford exerted her rightful influence in the home, insisting on punctuality at meals, washed hands and faces, shirts in shape, the children standing behind their chairs when mealtime came.

Dr. Stephen Olford speaks of his mother as "a mother for a time of crisis." His memories reflect the truth of this statement, showing

17

her to be at her very best in crisis situations. One time a lion broke into the mission compound, killing the family's favorite cow—the supplier of all their milk. Father Olford was very disturbed because cows in Africa were hard to come by. He was determined to get this king of the forest so he wouldn't cause any more damage. With a fellow missionary they built a tree house, then cleaned their guns, and climbed up into the tree waiting for the lion to come back to pick up the remains of the carcass.

That night it was bitter cold. Mrs. Olford couldn't sleep because of her concern for these two men. The villagers and the Olford family had been warned that no one was to venture out into the night, because any movement might be mistaken for the lion, and they would be shot. Suddenly jumping from bed, Dr. Olford recalls seeing her prepare hot chocolate, pouring it into a thermos, and then, in his words, "Mother sallied into the darkness singing a good old Gospel song, walking up the trail, carrying a lantern in one hand, a thermos in the other. Now that's my mother," he said, "fearless."

He relates additional stories that show her defiance of danger, such as "the forty-four day trip on a banana boat from the west coast of Africa to Portugal. A man was literally thrown out on deck to die, for he had infectious boils all over his body. He was put at the stern of the boat on a blanket, and food was pushed to him on a stick. Mother discovered it, and even with two boys at that time, and her husband to think about, she prayed about it and decided to give herself to aid this stricken man. Every day she went out to him, washed his sores, and fed him until he was cured. Before the end of the trip she had led him to Christ."

In 1935 the family unit returned to England to enable young Stephen to continue his studies. Then at the outbreak of the Second World War, Mrs. Olford assisted her husband in running a servicemen's center. The servicemen called her "Our Mum." Danger was everywhere, but she showed herself again to be a mother for a time of crisis.

At war's end, Stephen Olford engaged in evangelistic work throughout the British Isles, Canada, and the United States. It was during one of these crusades in the north of England that word reached him that his beloved father had passed away. Just prior to his death Bessie Olford asked her husband, "What shall I do? Stephen is in a crusade, as you know." The father's reply was, "Don't bring him home. Tell the lad to 'preach the Word!' "

And this is what Stephen Olford has been doing faithfully ever since.

When in 1959 Stephen Olford and his family came to New York where he became pastor of Calvary Baptist Church in the heart of the city, his mother chose to remain in South Wales. A letter from her says, "Every Sunday morning as I hear Stephen broadcast over Trans World Radio, I remember him and his message, praying that the Lord will use him and the message."

Of this one who has meant so much to him and has been such a tremendous influence in his life, Dr. Olford says, "Mother was unashamed of tears—she wept over the salvation of souls, she wept over crisis situations, and she could weep tears of joy also—yet it was all perfectly compatible with her fearlessness."

For the world's women, mothers of tomorrow's children, Bessie Olford says, "My earnest prayer is that they may come to know the Lord Jesus Christ as their Savior, and that they may, in turn, lead their children to know him too, thus ensuring that the world may be a better place, and that the Lord Jesus may be glorified."

Just as Bessie Olford's son was used in his infancy to open doors for the gospel in African villages, so she has the joy of knowing God is using him now to open new doors in areas of radio, television, and wider outreach.

Someone has said that every time a man attains greatness, his mother shines in something more than reflected glory. In her I have sensed a mother who acted out her generosity, her kindness, her awareness of suffering, her love and beliefs in such a way that others, including her sons, would want to follow in her footsteps.

# Heather Brown Olford

## wife of STEPHEN F. OLFORD

As the "Ulster Monarch" steamship edged its way into Belfast Lough,* Heather Brown, standing on deck, turned from watching the rocky coastline and strained her eyes toward the dock. As she wondered who would be there to meet her, she sensed an inner glow at coming back home.

For Heather, home was Lurgan in Northern Ireland, a linen manufacturing town on the shores of Lough Neagh. Going home,

* In Ireland the bays are called Loughs.

20

therefore, meant seeing her parents, her brother and two sisters, and a host of relatives.

The ship being securely docked, the passengers began to disembark. Moving into the crowd, she noticed a familiar face next to that of her sister. Instantly she recognized it as belonging to Stephen Olford, a young man who had ministered in her home town the year before. Smiling with delight, she extended her hand in greeting and exclaimed, "Stephen Olford! How good to see you again! What brings you to Ireland?" He explained that he was in Ireland to recuperate from a recent illness and to rest before sharing in the Belfast Convention, at which Heather would be the pianist.

As a promising musician whose ambition in life was to serve God through her music, she had often accompanied the evangelist Tom Rees and his wife in evangelistic work and had played the piano at their center in Hildenborough Hall. It was during one of these conferences that Heather had opportunity to become better acquainted with Stephen Olford. She had long admired the young evangelist and was much impressed with his ministry. His messages were of personal help to her and made such an impact upon her that at one point she had even gone to him to discuss a spiritual problem she had encountered. She rightfully regarded him as a great Christian leader whom God was using mightily. She says, "I placed him on a pedestal in my thinking. There was nothing in our relationship that would have given me any indication that someday I would become his wife."

And this was quite true. Some years before when Stephen Olford became an evangelist, he struggled in his soul as to whether or not marriage was part of God's purpose for his life. There were many eligible girls seeking a husband, and he knew he had to settle this issue at the outset of his ministry. As he explains, "Girls want to be dated. How does a young man approach this whole matter and maintain an example in the Christian life? I came to the conclusion that the Word either spoke to this or the whole message fell down. So I did an in-depth study on the subject. Basically, it had to do with our Lord's reference to the Old Testament when he was asked about marriage and divorce—which I felt encompassed this whole question of love and courtship.

"God said, 'In the beginning . . .' God's concern, I discovered, is greater than our own. Adam could never have analyzed what

21

was missing in his life, for Adam had never seen a woman! It was God who saw that it was not good for man to live alone.

"Next, I saw clearly that there was the matter of sexual adjustment. When God explained to Adam what was lacking in his life, he must have acquiesced to God's will, or else God would never have imposed a woman on his life, for to have done so against Adam's will would have been an immoral act. God caused a deep sleep to come upon him, and Adam was prepared to rest in the will of God until God awakened him to the right partner. Only while Adam was asleep in the will of God could God create the woman that was suitable for him in every respect.

"Then, of course, there was the awakening—God's consummation of the love, courtship, and marriage, as it were. When Adam awakened, the woman that God brought him matched him perfectly. There was an affinity of spirit, soul, and body, for they had met in God.

"As far as I was concerned, this revolutionized my thinking. Having seen this truth, I decided I was not going to do any kind of exploring to find a wife; I was going to sleep in the will of God. And the amazing thing is that when you sleep in God's will, he puts a protection around you. Many young women could have broken into my life between the ages of twenty-five to thirty, but they were held off while I did the job God wanted me to do."

Thus it was that having met Stephen Olford on several previous occasions, Heather Brown held him in great respect; Stephen Olford thought of her as an unusually gifted young pianist. Her artistic capabilities had not escaped his discerning eye, neither, for that matter, had her sweet nature. If someone had asked for an opinion, he might have surprised them and himself by assessing her as possessing a compelling winsomeness and as being "a bonnie lass!"

Heather Brown was raised in a Christian home. At the age of ten she attended evangelistic meetings in her home town led by Tom Rees, and following a service one night she came home and knelt by her bed, with her mother at her side, and invited Christ to come into her heart.

While in college she experienced a brief spiritual tussle; yet, she was conscious of an awesome sense of God working in her life—which, indeed, he was! At that time Tom Rees again came to their community and preached on Romans 12:1–2: "I beseech you therefore, brethren, by the mercies of God, that ye present your

22

bodies a living sacrifice, holy, acceptable unto God, which is your reasonable service. And be not conformed to this world: but be ye transformed by the renewing of your mind, that ye may prove what is that good, and acceptable, and perfect will of God." Those verses went straight to the heart of Heather's tussle. "To me, the whole message was just this: if God had given me so much, how could I hold back my insignificant life? Mr. Rees counseled with me, and that night I gave everything over to the Lord. This resolved the distress of my heart concerning my future. Although I had been studying music, I realized that I would never be completely satisfied unless I was using my musical ability for the Lord.

"As a result of this encounter I was invited to join Mr. and Mrs. Rees in their evangelistic ministry and youth center at Hildenborough Hall. This opportunity to serve the Lord, coming when it did, met a deep need in my life at that time."

While Heather was assisting in crusade work as an accompanist, she felt the need for further musical training. As a result of reading a copy of *Moody Monthly* magazine and by coming into contact with a United Nations Witness Team in London—young people who had attended Moody Bible Institute in Chicago—she felt God leading her to enroll in this school where she could study music as well as Bible.

Petite and pretty, Heather Brown admits she had her share of admirers. Her friendships were many, but in her words: "There was always something that God seemed to be saying to me—this isn't the right man for you. I just knew that God had someone special picked out for me, and I was in no hurry. I was content to wait on the Lord."

The day came, however, when Stephen Olford became deeply restless. After real soul searching, he decided to go up into the Welsh mountains to wait on God for some answers. While there God clearly showed him, as he studied the Word, about his need for a life partner. He found himself questioning, "Well, Lord, who is it going to be?"

At this juncture in his life he became ill. While he was recovering from this illness, the doctor insisted he go away for a few weeks' rest. He wondered if he could recuperate in Ireland, prior to sharing with other speakers in the Belfast Young People's Convention. Arrangements were quickly made, and so it was that he found himself in Ireland at the time that Heather Brown was to arrive home. On the morning of her arrival, Heather's sister, Lillian, asked him if he would like to join her for an early trip to the Belfast docks. In his private devotions that morning Stephen Olford had read from the Book of Proverbs: "Whoso findeth a wife findeth a good thing." The verse had gone on to say, "and obtaineth favor of the Lord." That phrase—"obtaineth favor of the Lord"—was the healing balm he needed for the restlessness in his heart.

Before the convention was due to begin, the Brown family planned a day's outing to the beach. But for one reason or another each member of the family was unable to go, leaving Heather and Stephen to spend the day alone. The countryside had never appeared lovelier—the rugged coast, the beautiful glens, the hills and the mountains appliqued with thatched-roof cottages and stone-walled castles. But that day she was oblivious to the beauty of the countryside as her attention was completely diverted by what her traveling companion was saying. He was sharing with her all that was in his heart about the ministry God had given him.

Then it was Heather's turn to pour out the yearnings of her heart, and she began to talk about what her burden was too—her desire and vision to serve the Lord Jesus Christ through her music. She shared with him the dream of going to America, of attending Moody Bible Institute. Suddenly Stephen pulled to the side of the road and stopped the car.

As he now explains, "The jigsaw puzzle so perfectly matched that it was not funny. We bowed our heads, and I found myself praying that God would guide our lives. As I prayed I thanked him for Heather, for giving her to me, and accepted her by faith, so that I really proposed to her in my prayer. She followed with a prayer and did exactly the same thing. And when she finished, for the first time in five years I kissed a girl, and we were engaged at that very moment!"

There had been no courtship, no dating. God had brought them together and they recognized his divine leading and never once questioned this. Stephen Olford continues his account of what happened next. "We went back to her home and shared it with her people, and it was just thrilling the way they rejoiced. And that night I phoned my parents living in Wales and *they* rejoiced. We started with engagement, and our courtship continued in the United States for a year in tiny little breaks while she studied at Moody and I traveled the country."

Stephen Olford covered thirty-four thousand miles doing evangelistic work, much of it with Billy Graham and Youth for Christ.

24

The year was 1947. During that year Heather's studies were interrupted when Stephen became very ill and had to have surgery at Mayo Clinic. But once again at Moody she plunged into her studies with renewed dedication, knowing that she would not have the opportunity again, for plans had been made to return to Ireland to be married the following year. The return trip was made with the goodwill of all the friends in this country.

It was very romantic and thrilling how God brought these two lives together. Today, when the Olfords counsel young people, they do so with great confidence. The Olfords, knowing that God has the right partner chosen for them, counsel young people to wait for God to reveal his will. When he brings people together they will know for a certainty.

Not only were Stephen and Heather terribly in love, in their own words, "almost from first sight," but the spiritual impact that they have on each other is one of total dedication to a common cause—that of serving the Lord in evangelism.

"In times of distress and discouragement, Heather has always provided the inspiration and incentive to rise up and get going again," said this zealous man of God the day I visited the two of them in their charming New York apartment. It was said casually, but was a tribute spoken with a depth of meaning which his wife interpreted rightly as they exchanged tender glances.

On a memorable morning in August, 1959, Stephen Olford, his wife, and two sons arrived in New York to take up the ministry at Calvary Baptist Church in the heart of the city. Heather had made the adjustment beautifully to becoming the wife of one of Europe's most outstanding evangelists; now she was to face more days, weeks, and months of adjustment, as together the family sought to identify themselves with a new country, a new city, and a new church. But the people at Calvary showed such love, patience, and understanding that the days of trial paled into insignificance in comparison to the times of triumph.

Their experiences have been many and memorable—milestones that have brought glory to God in a constant outreach through the church and through radio and television. In 1960 Dr. Olford launched a television program called *Encounter,* which is now seen in color on some six stations across the United States. He has participated in conventions, crusades, open-air rallies, Christian Life Conventions, and many other events too numerous to mention— labors of love in which the Olfords have worked side by side.

Heather Olford describes her married life like this: "I knew that God, having given me a husband, intended my task in life to be that of loving and caring for him—making a happy home for him and the family we prayed God would give us. He led me into marriage, and everything else that would ever happen to me had to take second place. I knew that together God intended for us to serve him.

"As we moved from itinerant ministry into church life, our lives changed quite a bit; but the changes have been changes we have made together. The result has been real peace of mind as God has shown me ways of fitting my schedule into that of my husband's, thus making life easier and happier for him.

"The responsibilities of homemaking and caring for the children God has given us have been wonderful. Although Jonathan was seven and David only three when we moved to New York City, we were faced with some adjustments raising them in the city. But it is just a matter of calling upon God's grace and power; this is the art of adjustment. Many people have questioned, 'How can you stand to live in the city?' You don't ask questions when God is leading you, and we knew God was bringing us here and we knew he would help us to adjust.

"And so my part, from the very beginning of our ministry here at Calvary, has been to relieve my husband of concern for the children here in the city; therefore, when the children were younger I didn't attempt to do too much in the church itself. We live near Central Park, and often I would take them over there to play. We concentrated on family fun, and all of us have been drawn close together as a result.

"Both my husband and I like sports. We played ball together in England, quite a bit of tennis, and we have continued this as a family. Vacations have never been a problem, for we go where we can play and enjoy the out-of-doors. We like the ocean and enjoy the mountains. We swim, play golf and tennis.

"Since schooling in the city is a problem, we have felt compelled to send our boys away to boarding school. This was very hard for both of us, but my husband, realizing this, has been considerate and thoughtful.

"My husband is a disciplined and well-ordered man. I have learned if I can be this way, it also helps. This is the way, then, that we plan our lives. His day off is Monday. But if something comes up that we realize can't be helped, we determine together that we will make up for it another time. If we planned a whole day off together, and it turns out to be just one hour, then that one hour becomes very special. It is being together and understanding each other that matters.

"If my husband has an evening of counseling, I don't begrudge the time he has to give. I don't believe in sitting around feeling sorry for myself. I can always find something else to do!"

Mrs. Olford reads a great deal, and the wall of her study was well lined with choice selections of outstanding books. She handles her own correspondence, which is considerable. She does not have a personal secretary. Now that her sons are away at school, she is able to attend conventions with her husband. She still limits her outside activities, feeling that the pressures on her husband are such that he needs an uninvolved wife. At times she feels like his third secretary, but loves every moment of it! She answers the phone for him and assists in counseling when she can.

She believes rather strongly that churches should not try to fit a new minister's wife into the mold of any previous pastor's wife, and that every woman should recognize her own capabilities and do what she is best suited to do. She urges women to recognize their individuality to be what God created them to be and to leave the results with him. She recognizes that it helps when one's husband is in agreement with this philosophy—he doesn't expect more from his partner than she is capable of giving.

Mrs. Olford has taken an active role in the Women's Missionary Society and plays the piano at the Sunday evening church service. She sums up her convictions regarding one's talents in this way: "I believe that God's gifts are tremendous and are to be used for him. He has given gifts to the church, and when we realize what our particular gift is, then we have peace and satisfaction in our hearts as we serve him."

When asked what it's like living a kind of goldfish bowl life where you are being watched rather closely, Mrs. Olford says, "We don't think of it that way. We are the Lord's servants. There is a price for leadership, but we try to live at home before each other and before others what my husband preaches, so there is no pretense. Actually the goldfish bowl God is watching is us, and because what we are is much more important than what we do, therefore what we are before God is what really matters. At this moment I just thank the Lord for what he has done for us. I could ask for nothing more in this world than the excitement of knowing Christ and being in his plan for our lives.

As I was sitting in the beautiful living room of the Olford apartment, looking at the lovely Irish lady across from me, with her delicate features, deep-set eyes, and winsome smile, there was no room for doubt in my mind that she was speaking from her heart. The apartment itself gave evidence of the charming person that she is—from its bright green carpet, reminiscent, I'm sure, of the verdant Irish countryside, to its tastefully chosen furniture and special touches on walls and tables—truly a place a man would like to come home to.

On the occasion of the Olford's tenth anniversary at Calvary, a special souvenir edition of *Encounter,* the church's magazine, was produced. In it was a section devoted to "Our Minister's Wife." It read as follows:

> To you, Heather Olford, whose life in Christ is a constant challenge and blessing to us, the women of Calvary Baptist Church pay sincere and highest tribute. We give humble thanks to God, for only the life of "Christ in you" could account for the woman we see you to be.

> One of our Deaconesses writes, "Mrs. Olford personifies her husband's oft-recurring sermon theme, 'the Lordship of Christ in the believer's life.' And so you are to us, as she further states, 'the Ideal Pastor's Wife."

> We saw you first as one who had received careful training in discipline in perfecting your God-given musical talent; and as one who had dedicated that talent to the Lord for His service. We have been assured of the strength and depth of your spiritual life in many ways as we have come to know you and have sensed how much you care that Christ be exalted in our church and made known in the world. Only when the books are opened will we know how much your prayers contributed to the power and effectiveness of your husband's preaching. In fact, we often ask, "Are you the woman you are because of his preaching or is he the preacher he is because of your praying?" We have realized something of the outworking of your spiritual life in your faithfulness to our missionaries and your deep concern for them.

> We see the work of the Holy Spirit in your well-ordered life and wise social relationships; a friendliness with gracious dignity that we deeply appreciate.

> Another woman writes: "I've watched her, listened to her as she has chaired women's meetings, defined a point in a Bible

28

School class discussion, conversed with those in the church and those outside it, and always I've been impressed with her discretion and wisdom. I am proud to introduce Mrs. Olford as my Pastor's wife."

We see your wholehearted dedication to Christ in your untiring labors with your husband in the church, in the radio and television ministry, in your constant outreach to the lost, in the lives of your two fine sons and in many other ways.

One who works with you in the Women's Missionary Society sums it all up in the words of Proverbs 31:30b: "A woman who reverently and worshipfully fears the Lord . . . she shall be praised."

Many years ago God made very real to Heather Olford the words of John 15:16, "Ye have not chosen me, but I have chosen you . . ." As I have reflected on her life, I have come to understand why that verse should be so meaningful to her. When Heather Brown saw Stephen Olford on that dock at Belfast those many years ago and asked, "What brings you to Ireland?" she could not know that God had chosen her to be the woman behind a great man.

## Mary Lee Bright

mother of BILL BRIGHT

He stepped down off the bus, heard the swish-swoosh of the door as it closed, and watched as its taillights disappeared into the darkness. He'd stayed after school to practice for the class play. Darkness came early these winter evenings, and now he wished that he had left earlier. He stumbled in a deep rut, unable to see the way. Snow filled his boots, his fingers were getting numb, and his nose was cold. In fact, he was cold all over. How much further was it, he wondered. It was hard to tell in the dark.

Was that a light coming toward him? He strained his eyes to see, quickening his step along the rutted road. Yes, yes it was a light.

She was meeting him again! He'd told her not to do that. He'd be okay. No need for her to leave the warm house. A tear ran down the side of his face. Now the light was getting brighter; she was coming closer. He heard her call, "Is that you, Bill?" He answered back, "Yes, is that you, Mother?"

Mary Lee Bright, mother of seven, played no favorites with her children. Lantern in hand, she walked that rutted road countless times through the years to meet her sons and daughters when after-school activities kept them late. Her tender heart knew the fears a young boy or girl would have walking alone through the dark. One's imagination could play tricks, and she sensed their fears. Children need a light in the dark.

As she walked that Oklahoma country road that night, shoulders hunched forward against the howling wind, she thought: Bill—what a good son. He showed such signs of promise. Her friends all said, "Someday he'll be a preacher." She didn't doubt it one bit. She knew he'd do something special with his life. She couldn't help wondering what that would be. At times she wished for a light to see into the unknown future for her children—just a glimmer to allay some of her fears.

Just as quickly as that thought came she chided herself: Mary Lee Bright, you have a Light! Indeed she did have! That Light came into her own life as a young girl of fifteen. It had never stopped shining, showing her the way.

Mary Lee Rohl was born into a devout Christian home where seven children received early nurture and consistent Christian training. "Every time the church doors were opened, some of us were there. Sometimes we would go by horseback, but we were there. On one occasion a revivalist came, and I felt compelled to go to the altar. When I reached home, I knelt by my bed. 'Lord, I know you can help me. I want to feel your presence.' I never doubted my experience after that prayer."

Upon graduation from high school, Mary Lee went on to college to become a teacher.

Waves of homesickness engulfed Mary Lee when she left to take her first teaching job. But it was here that she met jovial, good-natured Dale Bright, proprietor of the local butcher shop.

She recalled that event as we sat in the comfortable plainly furnished living room of Dr. Bill Bright's parents at Coweta, Oklahoma. Bill Bright, founder and president of Campus Crusade for Christ International, leaned back in his chair and laughed heartily

31

at his parents reminiscing. This man who is invited to lecture in famous centers of learning in leading countries of the world had received his early learning from these two. Now he regarded his mother with tenderness befitting a great man who attributes what has happened to him as an answer to his mother's prayers.

In 1921 Dale Bright moved his family to a 3,284-acre ranch, five miles from Coweta, Oklahoma. That same year on October 19, their sixth child, Bill, was born. A stillborn baby had been born to Mary, preceding Bill's birth. When it was learned she was expecting another child, there was fear for her well-being. She had been near death before, and it appeared this pregnancy would be the same. Mary Lee was determined to carry the child and retreated into her Bible and prayer with a devotion she had never experienced before. "I just searched the Scriptures and prayed without ceasing. As I did this, the strong feeling came over me that I would be all right and so would the child. It was at this time, before he was born, that I dedicated him to the Lord. And do you know, he turned out wonderfully well!" Mary Lee Bright turned her head, her eyes looking with pride at her son. "Look at him now," she motioned in Bill's direction.

The older brothers and sisters welcomed the new baby and proceeded to do a good job of caring for him. Mary Lee's daughter Florence was raising ducks but was having difficulty. When she would put out a pan of water for the ducklings and come back to them later, she would find one or two of them dead. By this time Bill was toddling about. When Florence came to her mother weeping because of her ducklings, her mother wisely said, "Now hide and watch the next time you put the water out. Maybe you can discover what's happening."

Florence dutifully obeyed her mother. Soon little Bill came along, picked up a downy little duck, squeezed it lovingly to his face, then put it down. Florence watched, horrified! Her baby brother was loving the life right out of her ducklings. For this he was soundly reprimanded, but it was one of the few times he required really stern discipline.

Another sister, Jo, recalls a trick Bill pulled on her many times: "We would get off the school bus, and I'd start walking in a hurry. Bill would say, 'Jo, slow down so we can walk and talk together.' I knew it was a trick, but I'd fall for it everytime just because I liked him so much. When we'd get near home, he'd hurry up and beat me home. He knew Mother would have something freshly baked waiting for us!" It was true. Mary Lee Bright liked nothing better than to bake goodies for her family and to surprise them when they came rushing in from school. It was a closely knit family with unbreakable cords of love and loyalty that exist to this very day. She was the first person up in the morning and the last person to go to bed at night; yet her children never recall hearing her complain.

Often she would speak to her children about the love of God and his faithfulness. "I look forward to going to be with the Lord someday," she would say. Bill would look at his mother with respectful awe, yet feeling a little hurt not understanding: Wasn't she happy with them? He had not yet turned his own life over to his mother's Savior.

Her interest in the children's well-being extended into nightly study of their school homework with them. Her own proficiency as a teacher was an advantage to her children. When they brought home books on which they needed to report, she would say, "Let's read aloud so we can all enjoy them."

To these reading aloud times Bill attributes his own great life-long interest in reading and the fact that he learned to read while still very young. The Bright home had a good home library with historical and research books in addition to excellent encyclopedias. The niceties of life were not nearly as important as good literature.

The children were encouraged to share responsibilities, working on the ranch, earning money and buying some of their own clothes. That was good training. They were taught that the possession of things as such was not important. When the children would experience failure in a venture, Mrs. Bright was right there to cheer them on.

No barriers or generation gap existed between Mother Bright and her teen-agers. "We would discuss anything with mother," recalls Dr. Bill Bright. She was accessible and engendered in her children the desire to share confidences. They knew she would understand. "She trusted us," Bill continued, "and we weren't about to let that trust down or to disappoint her in any way. We wanted to be worthy of that trust."

Campus Crusade for Christ has a firm policy that no staff member is ever to repeat a joke or tell a story that reflects in any way on any race, color, or minority group. Its founder and president attributes this deep conviction to his mother's training. "Mother taught us that we were no better than anyone else, regardless of the color of their skin. We have no reason to be proud just because we are white, to feel superior, for in the eyes of God the color of a man's skin is unimportant. Mother had many favorite little sayings which she would quote at appropriate times. We were not allowed to indulge in any kind of prejudice, and if we were tempted, Mother would correct us by saying, 'But for the grace of God, there go I.' "

Great freedom of expression within the home encouraged Bill to dream big dreams and to develop a mental attitude which welcomed a challenge.

One summer Bill declared his desire to go off on a hitch-hiking trip across the country in order to gain experience to write a book. Now he looks back upon this side venture as a foolish thing to do, but Mrs. Bright did not attempt to dissuade him. "I put him in the Lord's hands and left him there. I knew God would take care of him," she explained.

When Bill went off to college, he left knowing that he was expected to pay his own way. "I washed dishes on campus for three hours a day for my meals, scrubbed floors and walls of rooms for my room in the dormitory, and had a laundry route which provided generously for extra income. These experiences caused me to mature rapidly and helped me more than my studies. You forget many of the things that you learn through academic pursuits, but some of those hard experiences stay with you forever. Mother had instilled into me true values and the worth of honest labor."

With the bombing of Pearl Harbor, Bill was determined to get into the service. He left home early one morning to volunteer. That evening the family was preparing to go to a school meeting and someone said, "Where's Bill?" Mrs. Bright replied that he'd planned to spend the day with his grandfather after going down to the local draft board. When she heard a noise upstairs, she decided to investigate. She found her Bill. "He was lying on his bed, just all broken up. I sat down beside him and asked him to tell me all about it. When he was younger, he had a bad ear infection. It left him with a perforated eardrum; as a result they would not accept him for any branch of the service." She comforted him, and then said some prophetic words. "Bill, the Lord has saved you for another service for him."

But Bill Bright could not accept that at the time. Shortly thereafter, he left for California, feeling confident that there they would accept him for the military service. But such was not the case. He was rejected from the service even in California.

By 1945 Bill had become well established in his own business in Hollywood, but something much more important happened to him. Through the ministry of the pastor of the First Presbyterian Church of Hollywood, Dr. Louis Evans, and Dr. Henrietta Mears, director of Christian education, Bill received Christ as his Savior and Lord.

When Bill became a Christian, he phoned his mother long distance and asked her to come and see him in California, because he had something important to share with her. "I remember her sitting in a big chair in my apartment, and I took her hands and said, 'Mother, I want you to know that I have dedicated my life to the Lord.' That's when she told me that she had dedicated me to him even before I was born." Tears filled the eyes of mother and son these many years later as they remembered that precious moment when a praying mother saw her prayers answered.

It was no surprise to Mary Lee Bright when Bill wrote telling of his love for Vonette Zachary, a hometown girl. On December 30, 1948, she acquired Vonette as her daughter-in-law.

The vision for Campus Crusade for Christ came in 1951. Indeed, his mother's prophecy had come true—the Lord had saved him for another service. But little did she dream that it would be a service that would have a world-wide impact. (The story of the founding of Campus Crusade for Christ is told in its entirety in the book *CAMEOS: Women Fashioned by God* where Dr. Bill Bright's wife's story is related.)

Today the man who directs a staff of several thousand workers who minister to students and laymen all over America and in more than half of the major countries of the world, says with deep emotion that the greatest influence of his life has been his mother's life and prayers. "She is the most godly person I know. She is quiet and self-effacing, but by her attitude and actions demonstrates a rare Christlike quality. Mother's life is characterized by commitment to Christ, a selfless spirit, a life of prayer, and a life in the Word. She wants no credit, glory, or honor. She loves Jesus with all her heart and has lived an exemplary life."

When asked what was the most important contribution a mother can make in the life of her children, she replied, "To train our children in recognition of the true values of life—to love God and enthrone Christ in our hearts. If we can teach our children to live close to him, then they need have no fear of what comes into their lives because God is in control."

Her gentle spirit showed in the concern she expressed for women of today. "I have deep compassion for women who are complacent about life. If they lived according to the teachings of the Word of God, mothers of today could change the world through their influence on the lives of their children. Too many women are going on their way in a complacent manner, not interested in the welfare of their children, more concerned about themselves, the pleasures of life, and the acquisition of things. We need dedicated women— dedicated to the cause of making Christ known."

Because of her own dedication, the world is seeing Christ in the lives of the men and women involved in the ministry of Campus Crusade for Christ which had its beginning with Mary Lee Bright's son. Christ is being made known by them in fifty countries; ten thousand staff members are expected by 1976. Prayer ascends around the clock daily that the Great Commission will be fulfilled by 1980. "All great spiritual revivals have been preceded by prayers," Dr. Bright says. "My own realization of the importance and magnitude of prayer can be traced to what I have seen and learned from my mother whose life has been characterized by prayer. Nothing encourages me more than to know that this very day my mother is on her knees praying for me, and that this evening she and my dad will remember me and the ministry of Campus Crusade for Christ in prayer."

I carried with me that day from that humble country home the memory of an angelic mother, the wrinkle laugh lines showing on her face, surrounded by gray-white hair, her work-worn hands folded quietly in her lap. There was a dear, sweet look on her face and I thought to myself: Yes, children need a light—a light in the dark, in the darkness of this world and this present age—and mothers like Mary Lee Bright can provide that kind of light.

# Nancy DeMoss

### wife of ARTHUR DeMOSS

"Nancy has a rare combination of talents—she's imaginative, flexible, a good hostess, a wonderful mother, a tremendous wife, but most important, she is yielded to the Lord."

The man speaking with such pride and obvious devotion was Arthur DeMoss. After thirteen years of marriage (at the time of this writing), Nancy and Art were still holding hands, sitting close together, looking at each other that special way known to lovers. One had the feeling theirs was a beautiful relationship.

It was February 14, Valentine's Day, and a radiant Nancy had met me. Pinned to her burgundy red knit suit was a pin. "Look what

37

Art had on my pillow when I woke up this morning!" She pointed to the piece of jewelry—two gold hearts entwined together with a single beautiful diamond in the one. "He purchased it before we left home and saved it until this morning." The significance of the intertwined hearts was meaningful; no wonder Nancy DeMoss was aglow. It wasn't the gift alone. It was the message it conveyed from her beloved Art that was important.

Later, in the busy lobby of the Campus Crusade for Christ Arrowhead Springs headquarters, where an Executive Conference was being held which had brought Art and Nancy to the West Coast, we saw Art crossing the lobby to meet Nancy for a brief moment, and her lips moved in a silent, "I love you!" I was beginning to understand what would prompt Arthur DeMoss to speak so touchingly of his wife. I knew that in Nancy we had a good subject for a woman behind a great man.

It takes two to make a marriage a success. Nancy and Art would attest to this. It also takes work, sacrifice, patience, understanding, forgiveness, self-discipline, a supreme concern for the other, and an ability to give and receive love. She is a busy mother with their six children, and he a busy husband as founder and president of the National Liberty Corporation, National Liberty Life Insurance Company, and National Liberty Foundation, in addition to his many other interests. Yet Nancy and Art each contribute in such a way to their marriage that the meaning of 1 Peter 3:1–12 is beautifully exemplified in their relationship.

But their relationship had a beginning fraught with frustrations, misunderstandings, and more than its share of heartaches. Perhaps this has contributed to cementing their marital ties into the more perfect union of two hearts as one—this, and their mutual desire for Christ to have the supremacy in their individual experiences and in their home.

Nancy Sossomon of Charlotte, North Carolina, was blossoming into young womanhood when she first met Arthur DeMoss. He was speaking at a Christian Businessmen's Dinner, and Nancy, because of her exceptional musical ability, had been asked to sing and accompany another singer. She was not a Christian at the time, and on the way to the dinner they made fun of what lay ahead. "How are we ever going to sit through a boring religious talk?" This was the theme of their discussion, and they couldn't wait for the meeting to end. Nancy recalls that they were relieved to get away afterwards and laughed all the way home.

Less than a year later Nancy was asked to sing at the same CBMC affair. But in the intervening time something happened that changed her laugh of scorn to a cry of discovery.

It has been said that when God is going to do something wonderful, he begins with a difficulty; but if it is going to be something very wonderful, he begins with an impossibility! Nancy Sossomon, a bubbly, blonde, brown-eyed teen-ager, qualified well for the description of impossible!

Music was her consuming passion. She began studying piano at the age of five; but as early as eleven her interest turned to voice. At the remarkable age of fourteen she had won the vocal scholarship awarded by the North Carolina Federation of Music Clubs. She was the youngest singer ever chosen to appear as soloist in Handel's *Messiah* with a symphony orchestra. It was a promising start that was to lead to an impressive but brief vocal career before marriage. While her musical talent might have been impressive, her actions as a teen-ager left something to be desired.

Because her musical ability thrust her into contact with older sophisticated people, and because she gave the appearance of being older than her age, Nancy was discovering that she had not learned how to cope with life and the experiences she was facing. Life for her at sixteen seemed purposeless. She was disillusioned with the adults with whom she associated and she thought: "If this is all there is to life, I just can't stand it. These people don't have any purpose or direction. If this is what it's going to be like for me, I feel like I'm washed up right now!"

God had been working behind the scenes, though Nancy was not aware of this. It was her junior year in high school, and because of her heavy schedule of music, she wanted to choose an easy load for school work. In looking over the electives she noticed a Bible course. She explains: "I had no intention of studying the Bible, though I had always had something of a desire to know God. The course appealed to me as an easy elective." The teacher, Rose DuPree, was a godly woman who set about at the beginning of the school year to have her students memorize two verses of Scripture from the New Testament each week. By the time October rolled around and Nancy was faced with the disenchantment of life, she had a month and a half of verses memorized in her head, though not in her heart.

Now, totally disillusioned, bitter, and in utter despair, ·Nancy made three appointments with local religious leaders. On three succeeding days she walked into the offices of these people to seek help, stating her desperate need and wondering if God could solve her problems. She received no help and left each time—a weeping sixteen-year-old.

Nancy got into the family car and drove to the chapel of a church where she was featured soloist. She went inside, still crying. After awhile she stopped crying and, with no particular reason in mind, walked up to the altar, climbed over the little rail, and started thumbing through the big pulpit Bible. Someone had underlined in red many verses that had been meaningful to him. Nancy explains: "I began to find these verses that I had been memorizing in school, and they were all salvation verses. God just started using those verses, and it was like I was hearing them from my heart. No one had ever told me how to become a Christian, but there it was—in the Bible, John 14:6, 'Jesus saith unto him, I am the way, the truth, and the life: no man cometh unto the Father, but by me.'

"I was looking for a way and another life, and it really dawned on me that here was the answer. I cried out for God. I remember standing there alone back of the pulpit. Suddenly I was on my knees telling God I wanted him, that I knew I needed him, and that I wanted my sins forgiven. I asked him would he, could he give me another way of life. And when I went out of there, I was a new person. I had gone into the chapel distraught and at the end of my rope. I hadn't seen anybody; yet I knew God had done something for me."

As a result of her remarkable conversion experience Nancy now says, "I have always had the deepest respect for the *power* of the Word of God." God really had done something for Nancy, and her life began to show it. The Bible tells us we are to tell others, to confess what Christ has done for us. This Nancy did, going to the teacher of the Bible course at her high school. The teacher became very helpful to her young student, and Nancy's life was completely turned around.

Nancy was her father's darling, and so, in her own uninhibited way, she began sharing with him and her mother what was happening to her. Her father, however, wasn't sure he liked the change.

Now, less than a year later, Nancy was singing at the CBMC dinner where once again Arthur DeMoss was speaker. This time she was impressed and afterwards, instead of making a hasty retreat, went up to him. "You know," she said, "we have the most

40

exciting thing going on in our high school. Kids are coming to know Christ just right and left. Would you come and speak?"

When Art DeMoss came to the school later in April of that year, Nancy saw many of her fellow students accept Christ as their Way of Life.

The story of Art DeMoss's life before and after his encounter with Christ would make any audience sit on the edge of their seats. As a successful young insurance executive Arthur DeMoss was changed overnight from a man interested only in the pursuit of money and pleasure into a person concerned about his fellow-men and their real selves. Though he drove Cadillac convertibles, gambled, drank, and enjoyed the company of women, in his heart Arthur DeMoss was rootless and dissatisfied. While living in his parents' home, he maintained upstairs two phones which kept ringing as he handled ten thousand dollars a day in horse racing bets for people in the area of Albany, New York.

He describes his mother as a small, vivacious, godly woman who read the Bible constantly. "She needed all her virtues, for she had a real cross to bear when it came to me," he explains.

*The Racing Form* was the gambler's bible, and every day Arthur would drive into town to buy a copy. One day while returning home he noticed that Hyman Appelman, the evangelist, was holding revival meetings in Albany. Before becoming an evangelist Appelman was a successful lawyer. This intrigued Art DeMoss, and his curiosity was further piqued by the fact that the meetings were being held in a mammoth converted horse stable. The idea of horses and religion under the same roof made him chuckle.

Art DeMoss went to that meeting, incredible as it may seem; and as the evangelist talked, Art found himself agreeing with the concise, logical presentation. His resistance vanished, and at the conclusion of that meeting Arthur DeMoss was on his feet, walking into a new life.

Was it any wonder Nancy Sossomon was impressed and wanted her classmates to hear this man? All of that had happened to Art DeMoss in October, 1950. Now, several years later, he was so successful in business that he traveled across the country, speaking out his conviction that Jesus Christ is the answer to all the problems of life, both for the individual and the world. At the age of thirty-three Arthur DeMoss was more successful than most men will ever become in their lifetime. Total premium value written by his general

41

agencies (he owned a number of them in various states) was about a million dollars a year.

Christianity had given him a different standard of values, however, and rather than being dazzled by his success, he had determined to use the advantage of having the financial means as an outreach for the Lord.

Arthur DeMoss saw in Nancy Sossomon an intensely serious young girl and instigated an attempt to get to know her better. Was it mere coincidence or God's planning that had Art staying with the Vernon Pattersons in Charlotte, who lived a block away from Nancy's home? A dinner meeting invitation was extended to Nancy where he was to be speaker. Nancy's plans for that evening found her attending another meeting, unable to accept Art's invitation.

When Nancy came home that night from her meeting, she found a note stating that the gentleman who had spoken at the school had called and wanted her to return his call before she retired that evening. Nancy's family had already gone upstairs, so she picked up the phone and just as quickly put it back down. In a few moments she was pressing the Patterson home doorbell.

The next several hours Nancy spent in the Patterson living room talking to Arthur DeMoss. He brought out some Christian books. It was the first time she was introduced to Christian literature like that. She will never forget his opening Tozer's book *Root of the Righteous* and reading portions of it aloud to her. They prayed together, and then he asked her, "Nancy, what do you want to do with your life?"

She told him the only thing she wanted to do was to sing professionally. Arthur DeMoss challenged her at that point. "Do you really know that this is what God wants you to do?" Nancy had never thought of that. She had already won a scholarship to Drake University in Des Moines, Iowa, where she planned to enter in the fall. When Art mentioned the possibility of her considering attendance at a Christian college, she politely demurred, stating her feeling that such colleges just wouldn't have the voice teachers worth studying under. Her ignorance was showing, and promptly he defended the Christian colleges and told her that this was not the most important consideration.

Nancy didn't appreciate that phase of their conversation. It made her slightly uncomfortable but she had already developed a tremendous respect for him and felt drawn to him. When Art glanced at his watch, they were both astonished at the lateness of the hour—never had time flown so fast for both of them—and he offered to walk her home. That was the beginning of their interest in each other which was to go through some heartaches and misunderstandings before their relationship culminated in marriage.

She had no idea that Art DeMoss was the financial success that he was. In her words, "I wouldn't have known if he was making five, five hundred, or five hundred thousand dollars." Nancy's father did not approve of their interest in each other. He called Art DeMoss a "religious fanatic." At first Mr. Sossomon was relatively tolerant of Art's seeing his daughter; then he became openly irate and did all in his power to thwart the romance.

As Art traveled across the country, he would send letters and gifts to Nancy. Whenever possible Nancy's father intercepted the mail. "It was a very traumatic thing in our house, but God was very real to me and had really done something within my heart when he saved me. I was totally dependent on him," Nancy reflects.

When Nancy went to college at Drake, she received the correspondence and gifts from Art with joy and eagerness. Soon Art began phoning her, but once again the pressures started mounting —this time from friends and professors who felt she would be ruining her career to think of marriage at this stage. Friends tried to intervene, and again Nancy's father objected. Nancy was torn. Part of her father's objection arose over the fact that Art was some years older than Nancy. This went on for a period of many months, finally resulting in Nancy's returning a ring Art had given her. It was during the next summer when Art came to see her at home that the situation straightened out and they realized they were definitely in love. Together they prayed and sought God's leading.

That fall Nancy went to New York City to study privately under Samuel Margolis (Jerome Hines' teacher). This also brought her closer to where Art was living. That November 30, 1957, they were married at Fifth Avenue Presbyterian Church. To Nancy's surprise and joy, her parents showed up on the day of the wedding, and her father gave her away.

Thus began the most exciting and happiest days of Nancy's life. Art took his bride to Cuba and the British West Indies for their honeymoon, where he spoke to as many as ten thousand people a night in gospel services. He helped enroll forty-eight hundred in a Bible correspondence course, following their decisions for Christ. Art took great pride in his Nancy's singing and insisted that she continue to study music. Together they had decided they would have no children for the first five years of their marriage, but Nancy explains what happened: "The children started arriving and I stopped studying!"

Did Nancy experience misgivings about this? For the young high-schooler who had told Arthur DeMoss that all she wanted to do was to sing professionally—what did this do to those dreams? Nancy confesses to some adjustment in her thinking and of facing some struggles. "I was real young when we got married, and all of a sudden I found I had to cope with one, two, three—before you knew it six children—and a busy executive for a husband. I had just not lived long enough to know how to handle all of this. Though I was very mature in some ways, I wasn't in others. Art has a fantastic drive and real capacity for lots of work and many different projects at the same time. I had come from the South and was easy-going and disorganized; he was so organized and efficient. I felt guilty for a long time that I didn't have the same drives Art possessed and would berate myself, thinking Art is down at the office going through all those mental gyrations and what am I doing? There I was lying down, resting. I'd jump up and get busy. But I prayed about it, too, and then it was that God gave me the realization that he hadn't made me like Art, and I was to be what I was—a wife and mother."

Today Art and Nancy DeMoss live with their six children in a large English Tudor home built a half-century ago and surrounded by nine acres of rolling lawn and gardens in Villanova. Nearby, in Valley Forge, stand the buildings which house the National Liberty Corporation whose founder and president, Nancy's husband, is nationally recognized as a marketing genius.

What is generally less known is the fact that the first clerical functions associated with the original business known as DeMoss Associates were performed at the table in their breakfast nook in East Orange, New Jersey. Later it was decided to move to the Valley Forge area, where it soon became apparent that this was not to be a one-man, one-woman business.

Art DeMoss launched National Liberty Life Insurance Company under the slogan: "Special Protection for Special People." Those who could benefit from his far-sighted plan were to be that group of citizens tied together by only the slender thread of abstinence. This rising young executive himself would never have qualified for such insurance in his younger days! But now, with Christ at the helm of his life, and with his unbounded energy, optimistic outlook, and understanding and encouraging wife, Art DeMoss was to forge ahead with sales and growth at an almost unbelievable pace. Today the total market value of the six and one-half million shares of stock of the National Liberty Corporation is in excess of two hundred million dollars.

The phenomenal growth of the corporation can be traced to the dynamics of mass marketing, which its founder recognized in the early stages of the organization, and to his single-minded concern that all business policies reflect his Christian convictions.

The new idea that had its birth in 1959 came fully equipped with a new name: The Gold Star Plan. To Nancy and Art it really began as a hobby and developed into a personal sort of missionary project to raise support for such organizations as Campus Crusade for Christ and others—the objective being to reach people for Christ in several different ways. She explains it like this: "We felt that through the proceeds of the business, through the business itself, through the ministry we could have among employees, and through efforts by mail we would have an evangelistic ministry. To accomplish this we used full-page advertisements in *Wall Street Journal, Fortune, Time,* and other periodicals, exposing business and professional men to the claims of Jesus Christ. This has continued, resulting in an ever-increasing volume of letters.

"Then we have a form of direct mail evangelism where we mail out tens of thousands of 'soul-winning kits.' We promised the Lord if he blessed the business, we would turn over all the proceeds to him. It has been absolutely amazing to us to see the way he has blessed!"

Since Art and Nancy began in 1959, twelve hundred insurance companies have started in America. National Liberty Life Insurance Company has been number one in profits, in revenues, in market value, and number one in growth out of the twelve hundred.

Policyholders are also remembered on their birthdays with special booklets. For several years a small record was sent with Nancy singing "It Is Well with My Soul," "God Bless This House," "I'd Rather Have Jesus," etc. accompanied by the Gold Star Chorus comprised of people of the company. There was also a personal message from Art wishing the recipients a happy birthday, but more important, speaking to them of the need for the second birth and the availability of God's peace.

Chapel programs in the office find the DeMosses bringing in lay men and women who speak once a week. Children of company employees are treated to a Christian camp experience each summer with all expenses paid. Hundreds of conversion experiences could be related with many entire families coming to know Christ.

There is also a foundation whose objective is to see the world evangelized in this generation. Nancy states, "It is not just some vague, nebulous dream, but we are working through existing Christian organizations, serving as a catalyst to effectively assist others in getting the job done. We do research, conduct seminars, get Christian leaders together, or mission executives, or translation leaders. We invite them at the foundation's expense to come together to meet where we have real heart-searching sessions and conferences to plan and discuss their objectives, what is being done, what their problems and needs are. We try to get such organizations to define their long-range goals and objectives. Then we try to assist them in perfecting a strategy to implement them."

As a result of this, the term "God's Catalyst" has become descriptive of Art DeMoss, just as National Liberty Foundation stands for real liberty, the liberty to be found in Christ.

Another project Art and Nancy do together is the yearly compilation of the Gold Star Family Album Annual, a beautifully bound book containing choice meditations, poetry, illustrations, and devotional thoughts. Then there is the quarterly version of this hardback edition that has over a million readers per issue. It is mailed free to all policyholders, the aim being for readability and heart appeal tastefully presenting the message of the gospel.

One would think that with all of this, Art and Nancy DeMoss would have more than enough to think about, but another phase of their life together is yet to be told. Once a month they hold an open house or garden party to which they invite "up and outers." Art explains it this way: "It isn't difficult to reach them. They've got everything and yet know there's still a void in their lives. . . ." Each gathering, in a relaxed atmosphere, has at its center the desire to present Christ. To accomplish this the DeMosses invite someone like Jerome Hines, or socialite Eleanor Searle Whitney, who then presents a message.

Nancy is the real catalyst in this endeavor. She shares this in various places across the country, and at the time of this writing was doing that very thing at the Campus Crusade Executive Conference. Here are edited excerpts from her message: "Some years ago my husband and I became convicted after reading in 2 Kings the question, 'What have they seen in thy house?' Isaiah the prophet had come to Hezekiah (who was exposing his wealth to the Babylonians) and asked him that question.

"We started thinking about all the people that we knew and about the place that was very dear to us—our home—the place that was so comfortable to us, but that we were not fully utilizing for the Lord. We decided to ask God to show us the way we could reach our neighbors for Christ in our home. He showed us that we needed to be filled with the Holy Spirit, that we needed to get a vision of the lost world, that we needed to develop a strategy to reach them, and that we must pray daily for our prospects—by prospects I mean candidates for Christ.

"You may decide just to have coffee and dessert meetings, or you may want a simple buffet. Then again you may choose to have an elaborate buffet or seated dinner. It can be as formal or as simple as you desire, but the main thing is for you as host and hostess to be comfortable in what you are doing. You need to be relaxed, winsome, and charming.

"Find a name for your affair if you can. . . ." (Nancy showed samples of the invitations she and her husband used, and the names they attached to their parties.) "Receptions and open houses are good pullers to draw people in. We have had summer luaus, barbecues, and picnics. Garden parties in summer are lots of fun and colorful.

"One word of caution—don't step all over your children to reach the world for Christ. God really showed me this, and so now I include them in the beforehand preparations. My boys will set up chairs, and the girls will help me hull strawberries—anything will do so long as they are somehow included.

"We have found it is better to have the dinner or dessert before the speaker. A time of fellowship and informality prepares your guests for what follows. Be certain you secure the right kind of speaker for your 'prospects.' If you are trying to reach business people, then get a businessman or professional person as your speaker. If they are bankers or investment people, you might try to get a Christian stockbroker. Use discernment and ask God to lead. Outstanding Christian lay men and women are all over the country who are willing to speak and do this kind of thing."

So successful has Nancy been at this type of outreach that she has entertained as many as four hundred people in their home. She says, "God will give you the strength to do great things for him. He will make up what you lack physically."

Not everyone can entertain that many people at once, but your guest list will grow. Nancy suggests you begin with your close neighbors. She also keeps a card file with the names and addresses of everyone who was invited to their get-togethers and tries to keep some record of who came and their interest or response.

To expand your guest list, she suggests you use the society section of your local paper; she has even gotten names and addresses off mail boxes! Your husband's business friends are logical people to invite. Nancy maintains that God will give the increase, and you will have no trouble knowing whom to invite once you get started. She also urges that you ask your Christian friends to help you, both in preparations and in follow-up.

When Art DeMoss said his wife was imaginative, flexible, and a good hostess, he was speaking from firsthand observation of their many experiences in using their home as an outreach for the Lord.

Writing the story of Nancy DeMoss was no simple task—the details of her life with Arthur DeMoss would easily fill a book. 1 Peter 3 in the New Testament deals with marriage relationships. In *The Living Bible* it is paraphrased to read: "Wives, fit in with your husbands' plans. . . . Don't be concerned about the outward beauty that depends on jewelry, or beautiful clothes, or hair arrangement. Be beautiful inside, in your hearts, with the lasting charm of a gentle and quiet spirit which is so precious to God. That kind of deep beauty was seen in the saintly women of old, who trusted God and fitted in with their husbands' plans."

If any wife has adapted herself to fit in with her husband's plans, one would have to agree that Nancy DeMoss has succeeded in that.

# *Mabel Anderson*

### mother of CONGRESSMAN JOHN ANDERSON

Destined for political greatness, John B. Anderson could not have been born to a more 'right' mother than Mabel Anderson. She was right for him in every way—a woman of faith, vision, honesty, determination, and great good sense—and who, by the grace of God, was able to inculcate in her son these great qualities.

Born in 1886 into a family of ten children, Mabel Ring learned early how to work, how to apply herself diligently to whatever task was at hand, how to get along with others, how to get along without material advantages; but supremely, she learned to trust in God. This faith has been an enduring quality in her experience.

Mabel's father was a farmer, living with his family outside the little hamlet of Stillman Valley, Illinois. The children walked two and a half miles to the one-room country school. Mabel enjoyed writing and cherished a secret dream that someday she would become a writer. When the country schoolteacher read her stories aloud to the class, she shyly beamed and felt encouraged. Her dream was not to be realized, but her love of expression was to be transmitted to her son John, who someday would woo and win the confidence of the people of Illinois who elected him to become their congressman.

When she was sixteen, her family moved to Rockford Illinois. Mabel enrolled in Brown's Business College, became skilled as a bookkeeper, and learned typing and Gregg shorthand.

Her husband-to-be, meanwhile, was being reared in Sweden. At the age of fifteen, he immigrated alone to this country. Stalwart and ambitious, unafraid, too, young E. Albin Anderson made his way to Rockford, where he had a sister living. Albin was quiet, but when he met pretty Mabel at church, a friendship developed that culminated in a lovely church wedding.

Into this marriage six children were born, three little girls who died at the ages of four, five, and seven and a half. Infant mortality was commonplace in those days, and pneumonia and scarlet fever claimed them as victims. The tragedy of losing three children only made Mabel Anderson into a more beautiful person. It tempered her. It sent her fleeing, as it were, into the Word for comfort. Her next three children, Helen, thirteen months older than John, then John, and William, three and a half years younger, were to benefit from the heartbreak of that experience which made a deep impact upon the family.

When John was born February 15, 1922, in the Rockford hospital, Mabel turned to her husband and said, "Let's name him after our fathers."

Mr. Anderson was in the grocery and dry goods business, a job which was to demand a great deal of his time. Because of this, Mrs. Anderson redoubled her efforts to provide the happy home atmosphere she knew their children needed.

John Anderson's recollections of his childhood are distinct. He worked long hours after school, on Saturdays, and during vacations behind the counter with his father in the store. "We did all the tasks together—putting up potatoes in peck-size bags, sweeping the floor, waiting on the trade, and doing all the unglamorous things that go into running a successful business." Young John's outgoing personality was an asset to his businessman father, and John worked hard and willingly at this until he left home to attend college.

As a child he did not require exacting discipline. "I could always reason with him," says his mother. "Wherever we went, I would say, 'John, you watch the others,' and I could depend on him."

Saturday nights were fun-nights in the Anderson home. "Dad had to keep the store open until late at night, and so mother had a custom of rough-housing with us children, playing games. She had a lively sense of humor. She would take a plain old brown grocery sack and draw a funny face on it and put it on her head. She was a real comrade to us as children."

Holidays were memorable occasions. At Halloween time she would put on a pair of her husband's old pants, stuff a pillow inside, and go out disguised with her three youngsters. Her husband would laughingly tease and call her "looney."

Christmas memories are unforgettable! "This was very much a family celebration. I still remember going to grandmother's house. Father had four sisters, and since they would come with their children, lots of cousins were around. It would start with coffee for the older folks, and then later in the afternoon we would have a certain kind of bread. Everyone would dip his bread into the kettle, a sort of fondue called *döpa gryte* (Swedish). Then we would have a huge Christmas Eve dinner with Lutfisk and other traditional Swedish delicacies, ending always with rice with almond. The one that got the almond would be singularly blessed," the congressman smiled warmly as he reminisced. We interrupted his reminiscing to ask if he got the almond. "Yes, yes," he said, "I think I must have gotten the almond many times!" He continued, "After that we would go into the living room, and my grandfather would read the Christmas story in Swedish. Then we would all get down on our knees and the grown-ups would pray. Sometimes it would get very late, and we would get quite restless. Our presents would be waiting for us at home, and we were anxious to get there! Yes, Christmas Eve was very special. Then on Christmas morning we would get up at four o'clock and go to the morning service at church."

His memories of school center upon the contribution one teacher in particular made to his education. "Mami Vincer, my fifth or sixth grade teacher, really knew how to goad you until she got through what she was trying to teach. I didn't really appreciate her until I

51

grew up and now know she was truly a remarkable woman. She encouraged us to read widely." John's mother knew what this teacher was attempting to do and wisely reinforced her efforts with encouragement at home. Mrs. Anderson was widely read herself and knew the benefits that could accrue from this habit. She determined that her children would become readers, likewise. She would also sit down and help her children with their homework and studies, patiently answering questions and explaining.

When Mrs. Anderson sat at the piano, her agile fingers performing piano magic, her small son would stand alongside amazed at their rapidity, delighting in the sounds. He was familiar with the old gospel songs she was playing and soon started singing. "That's good, John," she would say. She stopped playing and drew the young tot close to her on the piano bench. "Now, let's start again."

Recognizing a quality in his voice and a good ear for tone, the young mother encouraged him to sing every time she sat down to play. It didn't take any coaxing. Young John Anderson loved music and thoroughly enjoyed these sessions at the piano. Inevitably he'd be drawn to join her, and soon a pattern developed of mother accompanying and son singing.

That pattern was to continue until the day John left home for college. His mother saw to it that he received voice lessons, and soon they were performing in public. Local and area-wide churches, hospitals, sanitariums, and many other places invited the team.

Mr. Anderson was active in the work of Gideons, and John was frequently asked to be star soloist. "One time, on a Sunday night, we went to Garden Prairie, just a little village. The old sexton was pretty grumpy about even opening up the church on a Sunday evening because they didn't regularly hold services. When we arrived, there wasn't a soul in the church, only the little band of Gideons and their boy singer. Since no one showed up, we finally opened wide the doors, and I stood in the open doorway singing, while mother stomped harder on the piano pedals and pounded the keys. It worked! In a short time, we had a small audience." Mother and son laughingly recounted that incident some thirty-one years later. And against the living room wall the old ebony piano still stood, mute evidence showing the scars of the esthetic expression which it had provided for son and mother.

In high school he sang on an 8:30 radio broadcast called "Morning Devotions" in the Rockford News Tower over WROK. Reverend Elmer Johnson was the pastor. It was an enriching experience and made the mother-son relationship one of great closeness. Sacred music was a very important part of this family's life.

John had a natural bent for learning. He was inquisitive, and this seeking sent him on countless trips to the library as soon as he was old enough to read for himself. His mother's reading aloud to him and his brother and sister had infused into him a love for good books. "He didn't want just story books," his mother relates. "He wanted books about men's lives. I used to wonder, 'Now, why is he so interested in reading about these great men of history?' "

Anything that had to do with history, politics, and government became a consuming passion to John. He read avidly, much to the disappointment of his classmates. I'm sure many young ladies looked at this handsome young fellow, hoping for some attention, only to be disappointed by his seeming disregard and nose-in-the-books attitude. It wasn't that he was blind, but John had more important things than girls on his mind. "He was shy around the girls, but very sensible," claims his mother.

He was an honor student in school and possessed a keen memory. Very articulate, he became captain of the school debating team, which was a natural for him. Extemporaneous speaking and debating brought many loving cups his way. He liked best to debate on current political subjects. In 1939 the Lion's Club in the community heard him debate on the subject of the Anglo-American Alliance. A gentleman in the audience who was a very prominent lawyer of that day, and still is, was so impressed with John's ability that he kept tabs on the boy in succeeding years. Later, when John Anderson graduated from Harvard Law School, this lawyer called to congratulate him and gave John his first job in a law firm. Out of that his interest in politics grew.

That interest may have been developing, however, when John was a youngster. He liked to do nothing better than to take a kitchen chair, turn it upside down, and use it as a pulpit. His preaching proclivities tended toward one favorite text involving the beheading of John the Baptist. John's mother would turn aside so her son wouldn't see her laughing as he expounded his theme. Younger brother William served as usher, and sister Helen dutifully carried on as organist! His captive audience heard the same sermon over and over again!

"The other influence that my mother brought to bear on my life that has stayed with me was our practice of family worship, sitting around the table, with mother or father reading the Bible. Then we would all bow our heads, and everyone participate in praying aloud."

The family devotions extended over into after-mealtime reading at which time Mother Anderson would gather around her the children and read to them from *Hurlbut's Story of the Bible*. John had received this Bible story book when radio station WMBI (Moody Bible Institute) in Chicago had offered it to the child who sent in the best name for their Saturday morning program. "Actually mother thought of the name 'Morning Glory Club' but sent it in with my name. How we loved listening to her read!"

"Yes, they enjoyed this," the soft-spoken, gray-haired lady on the couch recalled as our visit continued. "John was full of questions—he wanted to know, wanted to understand. And when he'd pray, he always said just what was on his heart."

Spiritual perception developed in this home atmosphere. This combined with faithfulness in church attendance; participation in Sunday school, worship services, choir, and youth fellowship meetings stimulated John's thinking, and to this day colors his responses to issues which he faces in the political world.

This was vividly demonstrated on the day of Martin Luther King's funeral when Congressman Anderson stood in the well of the House and spoke without notes concerning the controversial Open Housing Bill. He said, "I would respectfully suggest to this House that we are not simply knuckling under to pressure or listening to the voices of unreasoning fear of that hysteria if we seek to do that which we believe in our hearts is right and just.

"I legislate today not out of fear, but out of deep concern for the America I love. We do stand at a crossroad. We can continue the slide into an endless cycle of riot and disorder, or we can begin the slow and painful ascent toward that yet distant goal of equality of opportunity for all Americans regardless of race or color."

The House burst into applause. Congressmen from both sides of the aisle went over to shake Anderson's hand. And the speech switched votes—something a speech almost never does. That day Congress passed the Open Housing Bill.

Later, Anderson was known to have told a reporter, "The decision was very prayerfully made. A verse kept coming to me—a passage from 2 Corinthians 5 in the Phillips translation: 'For if a man is in Christ he becomes a new person altogether. . . . All this is God's doing, for he has reconciled us to himself through Jesus Christ; and he has made us agents of the reconciliation. God was in

54

Christ personally reconciling the world to himself . . . and has commissioned us with the message of reconciliation.' Within the growing realization of the need for reconciliation between black and white in this country, I saw ever more clearly the need for Christians particularly to be the agents of this reconciliation."

Daily contact with Scripture has given Congressman John Anderson certain principles from which he has never deviated. Every morning his mother would take little memory verses from a box, hand them to her children, and help them to memorize these before going off to school.

*Christian Life* magazine (October 1969) said of him: "The popular Congressman from conservative northern Illinois farmland votes his conscience and has taken a dynamic leadership role. His future seems unlimited."

This "voting of his conscience" can be traced back to his home training where precept upon precept was taught with resultant honesty and genius that can only add to the genius which is America.

"Sunday was very strictly observed, and sometimes now I feel uncomfortable when I have to do some things that would never have been allowed as a child. I believe that we, as families, would benefit greatly by a return to these biblical principles," observes the congressman.

Mrs. Anderson did not envision John as becoming a preacher. She always did think he would be in politics and knew that becoming a lawyer was the first logical step in that direction. Upon graduation from high school they encouraged him to attend the University of Illinois. Competitive examinations in high school qualified John for the county scholarship. His master's degree was received at Harvard Law School.

"I'm sure my going to college was an answer to mother's prayers because we never had much of this world's goods," he says with a touch of tenderness in his voice. We were sitting in the homey living room of his parents where the interview took place. From time to time the phone would interrupt our conversation, and the congressman would rise to receive long-distance calls from Washington. His mother's eyes followed her tall, now prematurely gray, bespectacled son with evident pride. It was plain to see that the mother-son relationship which had been so close through childhood was still strong.

"How do you feel when you see your son on television?" I asked.

55

Her face lit up with joy. "Ohhhh," she said, drawling the expression out, as I had noticed was a little habit, "I think it's won-der-ful!" The way she said it left no room for doubt that this little woman, face wreathed in pleasant lines, regarded her son with respectful awe and great love.

The congressman had rejoined us, "Now mother," he said, leaning over to pat her folded hands. Turning to me he added, "Mother's attitude has always been one of encouragement."

During the war years John Anderson served overseas in the European theater. Every week this mother wrote long, interesting letters, putting to good use her typing which she had learned as a young woman.

In October of 1952 he was assigned to the Diplomatic Corps in West Berlin, and in January, 1953, the Andersons acquired a daughter-in-law when his fiancée from this country went to Germany to marry John. That summer the Andersons went to see their son and his bride in Europe, and together they drove to Sweden.

John's father had not been back to his native land since he immigrated to the United States. "It was a real thrill to see the old family homestead near Boros, in the part of Sweden known as Westergotland," reminisced Mrs. Anderson.

John Anderson first entered politics when he ran for precinct committeeman and was elected for his home town, Rockford, Illinois. After that he went to Europe for the State Department and didn't become politically active again until 1955 when, upon returning from Europe, he came back to Rockford to practice law. The incumbent state attorney was resigning, and upon the urging of friends John ran for that office.

A very spirited primary in April, 1956, saw five candidates running. John Anderson was not favored to win, but everyone worked very hard, including his mother. He did receive the Republican nomination for state attorney and went on to win that post in November, 1956. That was the start of his political career which has seen him go on to greater things.

The incumbent congressman of the Rockford area announced his retirement, and John Anderson sensed another opportunity. Again, in a crowded field of five, and not favored to win, he did go on to victory in the April primary and was elected to the House in November of 1960. He has been there ever since.

As the congressman has risen in prominence to the third most important position on his side of the aisle, his mother has viewed his work with humble pride. "I am happy about his work because he is honest and I know he is a Christian man. John has always gone the 'straight way,' " she says with gratitude. "We brought all the children up in the nurture of the Lord. We taught them to always tell the truth." Her simple, sweet beliefs lived out in daily experience before her children provided a workable Christian faith with which they could easily identify. It carried over into their adult lives and today the congressman from Illinois is recognized as a "national Republican, a man bent for leadership" by the people of this country.

Of his mother the congressman says, "One of the most vivid memories I have is of mother on her knees before God in the living room. She has been a faithful prayer warrior all her life. She has been uncompromising with a completely shining and radiant faith. She would say to us as we were growing up, 'Even if you don't always understand God's ways, take time to listen to his voice—read your Bible and pray, that's how God speaks to you—God will make it plain to you what he has in store for you.' The strength and consistency of her Christian character, living what she said to us, these have been my heritage."

This from Congressman John B. Anderson who has been quoted as saying: "Man is inadequate to deal with the situation (in the world) as he finds it on his terms. Unless we accept God's terms, unless we find some wisdom and some strength and some solace in our Christian faith, the whole thing is pretty bleak and despairing.

"Particularly as I have been exposed here on the national scene to national problems and have become really aware of the dimensions of those problems, have I had my own conviction strengthened that it's only as we look to our Heavenly Father for strength and grace and guidance that we are ever going to be able to come out of this thing whole. . . . What a 'happening' there could be if the love of God could truly rule the passions of men's hearts. . . ."

Behind such beliefs as this lie the still stronger beliefs engendered within the home where all real training of a man begins. Her kindly face reflects the serenity of her inner spirit, and I couldn't help thinking that, yes, she was the right mother of the man for times like these.

# *Anna Currie Criswell*

## mother of W. A. CRISWELL

It was Sunday morning. Anna Criswell's labor pains were closer together now. She knew the time for delivery was near. Childbirth was not new to her. In the next room her fifteen-year-old daughter, Edith, and twelve-year-old daughter, Ruth, were getting ready for Sunday school. Her husband was waiting nearby anxiously.

At exactly 7:30 the child was born. His loud cries came as a welcome sound and Anna smiled with relief. It was a boy. Her prayers had been answered! She looked up at her husband, "We have a son." He smiled and nodded his head. Every man wants a son, and from the sound of things this one had healthy lungs. He was crying lustily. Today that sister Edith recalls, "He weighed six pounds and was a lovely baby. We were really thrilled about him!"

It was December 19, 1909, when Wallie Amos Criswell entered the world. Was it somewhat prophetic that he should be born on a Sunday? This man who was to spend his entire adult life using his vocal cords to proclaim from the pulpit Sunday after Sunday should first exercise those healthy lungs on the Lord's Day. The man who twice served as the president of the 11.3 million-member Southern Baptist Convention membership has never ceased crying out fearlessly and faithfully with an unequivocal devotion and dedication that is vigorously vocal and vibrant.

From whom did he inherit his tenacity of purpose, this unswerving zeal to that in which he so firmly believes? One need not look far to discover the deep purposefulness which was so much a part of his mother's character and which she so successfully imparted to her son.

Fortitude and charity were never lacking in Anna Criswell's life, and they were to fall like a mantle on the shoulders of her son.

Anna Currie, as was her maiden name, may herself have inherited a determination and drive, a certain genius for making her dreams of greatness come true in the life of her son, from her progenitors. Born in Paint Rock, Texas, to a Civil War veteran and his wife, Anna was to hear from her doctor father many stories of the grim tragedies of this wild conflagration. Today remnants of the courageous Curries—a sturdy breed of people, fearless, persistent, and confident—are still to be found living where the Concho River pours into the Colorado River, not too far from San Angelo in Texas.

When Anna married Wallie Amos Criswell, Sr., she held high hopes that someday she would have a son, and that he, like her beloved father, would become a doctor. This was her dream and she taught the little fellow to say, "When I grow up I'm going to be a doctor, just like my grandfather."

But Wallie Amos, Jr., even at a very tender age, was dreaming other dreams. He enjoyed nothing more in his childish play than to preach to the neighborhood youngsters. And when his father, who was choir director of their church, got up to direct, Wallie would toddle alongside him, wrap one small arm around his daddy's leg, throw his head back, and sing as loudly as he could. Everyone in the church loved the little fellow, which wasn't surprising, and he in turn loved them. His sparkling personality was catching, and the men in the church called him "Judge."

Anna Criswell was a serious-minded young mother with an unfailing graciousness. Life had been handed to her with plenty of wrinkles, and she wanted the best for her children. How could she accomplish this?

She was thankful her children were so receptive to spiritual teaching—that prayer and the Bible were meaningful to them. Religious literature and many books in the home provided reinforcement for the teaching they were receiving from their parents and in the church.

The church itself was the focus of the family life—no services were ever missed. Early in his childhood Wallie Amos, Jr., felt God calling him to be a preacher. When Wallie was ten years old, Pastor John Hicks of Dalhart, Texas, came to the church to conduct services. The Criswells invited him to stay in their home. Wallie looked forward to what went on *after* the services—he knew they would come home, drink freshly churned buttermilk, and he could listen in on his parents and Pastor John!

At one of the final services when Hicks finished preaching, the invitation was given. The congregation began singing, "There Is a Fountain Filled with Blood." Anna Criswell turned to her son—she was crying. "Son, today won't you accept the Lord as your Savior?" Wallie answered, "Yes, mother, I will." He rose from his seat, went down the aisle, and gave the preacher his hand. Anna's tears flowed even more freely.

Was it about this time that Anna's dreams took a different turn? Did she then envision for this son a future as a preacher? She was pleased and thankful for the dedicated life he was leading. His activities away from home all concentrated on what was going on at church.

Anna was spared the woes of teen-age rebellion with Wallie Amos. If the local cowboys were whooping it up in the tiny town where they lived high on the northwestern plains of Texas, Wallie was not to be found among them. When he was troublesome, which was seldom, a good serious talking to accomplished desired results. The relationship, according to Anna's daughters, "was an unusually sweet one between mother and son." The parents did keep a leather strap handy and in sight. Anna believed the biblical proverb which states: "The rod and reproof give wisdom: but a child left to himself bringeth his mother to shame."

There were no theaters, no vaudeville, not even ball games or paved roads, but as Dr. Criswell today says, "No one ever visited the place where we lived; no one knew it existed—but the Lord was there. In a thousand ways that boys and girls miss today, I was enriched in the presence of the Lord."

Her forceful personality and unclouded perspective found Anna taking her two sons, Wallie and Currie (named for her family maiden name), into Amarillo where they could attend high school. Life on the farm was becoming increasingly difficult during the dry dust bowl years. The situation was lean, but not Anna's will. She was ambitious for her sons, and high on her list of priorities was a good education. If securing an education for them meant she would have to bake pies, take in sewing, and work in a garment store doing alterations, then do these things she would.

Wallie had received elocution and expression lessons in his grade school years. There were gold medals and silver cups to prove his exceptional ability. In Amarillo High he became the star debater for the school. Anna beamed with satisfaction.

But Wallie also showed a proclivity to some musical talent. Anna told him to choose an instrument and he could have lessons. The Amarillo High Band, the High Y Band, and the Amarillo Municipal Band after that had a new trombone player!

For his high school graduation gift Anna worked doubly hard to provide the money for a typewriter. It was a sacrificial gift, but she knew how useful it would be in the years ahead.

All through the years Anna had seen this developing desire in Wallie to become a preacher. Everything he read or did had this one aim in sight. Thus it was no surprise to anyone when Mrs. Criswell took Wallie Amos to Waco, Texas, and enrolled him in Baylor. She wanted him to attend the finest Baptist school that there was, and Baylor was her choice.

Anna's son excelled immediately. He was only seventeen when he was called, while attending Baylor, to be pastor of his first little church. In his words, "I went through school preaching and pastoring, thus helping to work my way through college and gaining valuable experience."

His parents, meanwhile, were living in Amarillo where his father continued in the barber business. It demanded long hours.

Wallie remembered his parents' admonitions that if one studied hard, worked vigorously, and acted on one's convictions, one could achieve one's aims.

Anna's unshakable faith, consistent prayer life, devotion to the Bible, and desire to talk to everyone about the Lord at every opportunity had made it easy for Wallie Amos to catch something of her wisdom and sane approach to living the Christian life.

When his days at Baylor were ended, young Criswell went on to Southern Seminary at Louisville in 1931. There he earned his Master of Theology and finally his Doctor of Philosophy degree. While in college he acquired a wife, and Anna a daughter-in-law.

Anna's face was now furrowed by the years and the hardships endured, but the early struggles seemed as nothing placed beside the greatness of Wallie's achievements as his mother saw him receive his degrees.

His college and seminary pastorates in Chickasha and Muskogee, Oklahoma, had given the young Dr. Criswell a running start, so to speak, on shepherding the flock of God, the duties, multitudinous responsibilities, and yes, the heartaches that can accompany the pastoral ministry. Plainly, he knew what he was getting into. But his life had never been involved in frivolous pursuits, but rather was characterized by the burning zeal of an evangelist and a compassion that knew how to cry. He found it easy to identify with others in their times of heartache, tragedy, and sorrow. All of this he had seen exemplified in his own mother's life—a mother who did not flounder uncertainly herself, but knew "the Way" in which she should walk and had showed that "Way" to her children.

When the world's largest Southern Baptist Church—the First Baptist Church of Dallas, Texas—called Wallie Amos Criswell to become their pastor in 1944, Anna Criswell folded her hands in prayer, interceding for her son. She knew that he was seeking God's guidance praying, as he always did, "Speak, Lord, for thy servant heareth."

Dr. Criswell accepted that call to become the tenth pastor of the world's most outstanding and influential Baptist Church on October 7, 1944. He followed on the heels of the eminent George W. Truett.

The youthful Criswell was not unmindful of the mammoth task facing him, following as he was in the footsteps of this magnificent leader. But he soon realized, even as his parishioners pointed out, that they did not expect him to follow in Dr. Truett's footsteps, but rather, they wanted him to make footprints of his own.

If anyone believed that this was possible, it was Anna Criswell. It was she who had recorded his first faltering footsteps, marked his progress, kissed his scraped knees when he fell, picked him up and sent him on his way with encouraging words once again. Yes, she had watched the toddler steps become the bouncy run of a child, the jaunty walk of a confident teen-ager, the change to the stride of a man. Never once had she doubted that God had chosen this son for a special work for him.

Her own footsteps through life had been along a road interlaced with joys and sorrows; she knew the footprints Wallie Amos would make in this new ministry would have their share of the same. Yet she knew that God was faithful; and when at age eighty-six she went to be with her Lord, she had the joy of knowing that these footprints of her son were being seen around the world.

# Morrow Graham

## mother of BILLY GRAHAM

As Morrow Graham sat in the audience of eighteen thousand people in Earls Court, London, England, she shook her head slowly from side to side, marveling. The mother of Billy Graham never ceased to be amazed at the crowds who came to hear her evangelist son. An ocean and two decades separated mother and son from the first sermon she had heard Billy preach, but the effects were similar.

Billy's mother recalled the scenes as she and her daughters, Catherine and Jean, and her second son, Melvin, talked with me in her home in Charlotte, North Carolina.

Morrow and her husband, Frank, had driven Billy to a little Baptist church about forty miles from Charlotte. It was Christmas time, and Billy was home from college. Morrow was considerably more nervous than her son. "I was just wet with cold perspiration," she confesses. "He was only eighteen or nineteen. I don't remember one word he said; I only know he was good, but awfully loud!"

That feeling was shared by Morrow's daughters, Catherine and Jean, and her younger son, Melvin. They remember sitting in Billy's audience for the first time and squirming a little uncomfortably, wondering if others thought Billy talked too loud and fast. Catherine says, "He came out like he was preaching to a thousand people —my, he *was* loud!" Jean, now wife of Leighton Ford, associate evangelist on the Graham team, explains: "At that time he'd been preaching at Diamond Park, a trailer park in Florida near the Bible institute he attended, and he spoke out in the open. I think he thought he was still in that open field!" But every member of the family was proud of Billy, if not somewhat awed by his forcefulness and the way people responded to his messages, even in those early days. Loud, yes, but convincing!

Billy's fervor right from the start was of such intensity that it is doubtful he could restrain himself in small or vast enclosures. But certainly no one in the family expected that the boy who had swung from the big trees in the yard, screaming like Tarzan and frightening the wits out of passing horses and drivers, would someday exercise those same vocal cords by thundering "the Bible says" around the world.

Curtis Mitchell, in his biography about Billy, recalls a philosopher's question of many years ago; he called it the most important query of all time: "How do you get a man out of a boy?"

Ancient philosophers wondered and biblical writers often put the thought to words. Job questioned: "What is man, that thou shouldest magnify him? and that thou shouldest set thine heart upon him?" (Job 7:17). The Psalmist voiced the question, "What is man, that thou art mindful of him?" (Ps. 8:4). Elsewhere in the biblical record the same question is asked.

But men begin as infants, develop into children, then teen-agers, and emerge as men. What happens in between is all-important in shaping the destiny of the man. Certainly it can be stated that the parent's life is the child's copybook; and the old Jewish proverb which says, "God could not be everywhere, and so he made mothers," is as fine a tribute as has ever been written about the influence of a godly mother.

When Morrow Graham called out the window, "Billy, stop making so much noise," or reprimanded him for his boisterous activities as she righted an overturned chair, or mopped up a bucket of milk he'd spilled on the kitchen floor, or tried to find out, "Now why did you throw that rock through that man's windshield?" she had no way of knowing her disciplinary actions were molding the man who would talk to more people about Christ than any man in history.

As she sat in the audience at the London Crusade in 1966 and shook her head in amazement, it was the natural reaction of a person who considered herself "just a little country woman."

Born February 23, 1892, in Mecklenberg County, North Carolina, and named Morrow by her father, Ben Coffey, she was never to live more than a few miles from the site of her birth. She explains her name this way: "It is an old family name, and papa wanted his last child to carry that name. Mother was forty-two when I was born, and papa knew I would be their last child, and so he wouldn't allow Mama to give me even a middle name. I was supposed to be a son, and when I turned out to be a girl, he wasn't about to change his mind!"

Country-bred and country-raised, Morrow, early in life, heard of the horrors of the fighting that raged between the North and South. The South was still smarting from that—wasn't her father, a one-legged, one-eyed Confederate veteran, living proof of the awfulness of that war? There were times when little Morrow wished she didn't have to listen to the stories; yet she thought her father was the smartest, finest, most honest man alive.

Ben Coffey had been shot in the left leg, and he lay on the battlefield several hours. While he was waiting to be taken off the field, a shell burst nearby, putting out his right eye. Tall Ben Coffey was someone to be admired by his daughters, and Morrow would go through life thinking he was a better man with his one eye and one leg than a lot of men with two. Today Morrow Graham attributes much of her famous son's vim and vitality to the same drive she saw in her father.

What did country girls do for entertainment those long years ago? Morrow and her two sisters looked forward to Sunday nights and the church service. This was the zenith of their week. They walked the two miles, singing, swinging their arms, skipping along the dusty road. Morrow's softly contoured face, delicate features, and long blond hair made her the object of admiration from boys. "My hair was curly," she says, "just like an old-fashioned washboard, wavy-curly, hanging way below my waist."

She went to the country school through the tenth grade. From her mother she learned to sew—a skill which would later supply clothes to her growing family in lean years. Nurture in the Bible was encouraged by her devout parents. Morrow, while a young girl, memorized much of the long 119th Psalm, and often she would go to her room, lock the door, and sit alone, reading the Bible.

When her father died, she and her mother moved from the family farm into the city of Charlotte where they lived with an older married sister. Life in the city was different, and the college work she took up was hard. She enrolled in Elizabeth College, riding the streetcar to and from. She studied piano, voice, and public speaking. Her southern accent, though strong, revealed a well-modulated voice and a thoughtful manner of speaking.

As pretty and charming a Dixie belle as one could hope to find, Morrow Coffey did not go unnoticed by young William Franklin Graham. But, then, neither did Morrow look the other way when Frank, as he was called, approached her at Lakewood Park, west of Charlotte, where she had gone with a group of friends from a house party. She and the five girl friends had been boating on the lake. "Could I drive you home tonight, Morrow?"

He was the answer to a maiden's dream with his black, wavy hair, and Morrow had already been praying about him. She says, "I had seen him two or three times and wanted to meet him more than anything; so I asked the Lord that if it were in his will, could I please meet that handsome young man! All the girls liked him and wanted to date him, but I felt strongly drawn to him." It was reciprocal—and it was in God's will!

Frank Graham may have been "grand looking," in Morrow's words, but he also had the best looking horse and buggy in Mecklenberg County. If today's young girls are impressed with the mini-sport cars the fellows drive, Morrow and her girl friends were every bit as impressed with Frank's sporty rig and his sleek, fast horse.

Frank spirited Morrow away from the park with a flourish that left nothing to be desired, the horse, head held high, kicking up its heels, leaving Morrow's girl friends watching enviously—choking on the dust! Morrow must have thought she was on a cloud! She walked on air all week after hearing his words, "Morrow, I'd like to see you again Saturday night." Would Saturday ever come?

Shortly after meeting Frank, Morrow broke an engagement to another young man, giving back his diamond. In her words, "When I met Frank, I knew he was the one for me, and that settled it!" The romance was to last six years before Frank Graham felt he was able to get married.

The immediate families and a few close friends saw Morrow and Frank repeat their marriage vows on October 26, 1916. Frank thought she looked like a fragile doll with her golden ringlets cascading around her face. Before taking his petite bride back to the family farm where they would live, Frank whisked her away on the train to Asheville where they stayed in a hotel and had a five-day honeymoon. A happy light came into Morrow Graham's eyes as she reminisced, clasping her slim hands to her breast, "Oh, it was *so* exciting." And then it was home to the farm, and work.

Frank had inherited a three-hundred-acre farm after his parents died. It was all that was left of the family estate which had been ravaged by the Civil War. Living with him were an older widowed sister and a younger brother. The sister was to live with Frank and Morrow for two years and the brother for seventeen. The first two years of their marriage, they had no water, electricity, or inside plumbing in the house, but Frank and his good neighbor, Mr. Ashcraft, decided to try to do something for their women folk. It was a joyous day for Morrow when the old wood stove could go. "Frank bought one of those big, black Westinghouse electric ranges. I thought it was the grandest thing on earth! And then the two men went to work on city water, and the other neighbors said it couldn't be done. My Frank had a way about him of getting things done, and in less than a year we had city water."

He had also determined at the outset of their marriage that Morrow shouldn't be concerned with the demanding job of maintaining a garden, and he certainly didn't have the time. Neither did he want her raising chickens. But Morrow did convince him to plant cornfield beans and tomatoes. It was not at all unusual for her to gather two and a half bushels in an afternoon, and her husband would bring them up later by truck. By eleven o'clock at night she would have them all strung and ready for canning early the next morning. At the end of a busy season, Morrow could count at least five hundred jars of home canned fruits and vegetables.

One afternoon Morrow walked a good half mile down into the cornfield. Her long blond hair was neatly wrapped around her head in coils of thick braids the way Frank liked it. Later she walked back to the house, carrying a half-bushel basket of freshly picked beans. Her back ached a little; and as she sat down in the kitchen, she wondered momentarily if she should have done that. At one in the morning Morrow awakened her husband. "Frank . . . Frank . . . I think you'd better go for the nurse." Morrow was having labor pains.

Sixteen hours later, at five in the afternoon, she delivered the child. "What date is it, Frank?" she asked. And his reply came, "November 7, Morrow." He weighed seven pounds and seven ounces and was all baldheaded. Now the old frame farmhouse would echo with the sounds of little William Franklin, Jr. He sounded like all other newborn babies, but his cries touched the new little mother's heart in a special way.

Four days later, early in the morning on November 11, 1918, the Grahams were jolted out of their sleep by bells ringing and clanging across the fields from town, and they wondered what it could mean. There was no radio to tell them that the guns had stopped booming across the fields in France and that the Armistice had been signed. World War I was over!

Eighteen months later Morrow gave birth to their next child, a girl, whom they named Catherine. Between baby Catherine and toddler Billy, Morrow had her hands full. Billy was a climber. And when he wasn't climbing, he was reaching or leaping. Eggs were innocently scrambled on the kitchen floor and plates pulled off the table. One moment he was a tow-headed angel in disguise, the next a not-so-gentle bulldozer knocking over everything in his way.

Four years later in 1924, son Melvin was born; and in 1932 daughter Jean completed the family circle. Those were busy, hard years. Running the dairy farm was demanding work, and Frank Graham put in long hours.

When Billy was four years old, his father took him by the hand and they drove into Charlotte to hear the famous evangelist Billy Sunday. Life for the Grahams was never quite the same. Sunday was a colorful and mighty preacher. Billy was awed by the gigantic frame tabernacle erected for the occasion. Thousands of wooden benches filled its cavernous interior, and sawdust lay thick on the ground. "Mama, it's in my shoes."

Billy was fascinated by the goings on . . . the singing was unlike anything he'd ever heard, quite a contrast to the psalm-singing he was accustomed to hearing every Sunday! But he was even more impressed by the evangelist who waved, shouted, climbed on the pulpit and the piano, and looked and acted more like a baseball player than a preacher! When little Billy learned that he was a former big league ballplayer, he was doubly impressed!

Church going after that seemed rather mild in comparison, but faithfulness in church attendance was a must with the Grahams. Billy relieved the long hours with heel-kicking and knuckle-cracking, much to the displeasure of his mother and father. He came to know the church building very well—every nook and cranny—the result of childish explorations while his parents were "after-church-talking" with friends and neighbors.

Billy seldom walked anywhere, always zoomed through the house, causing Morrow to catch her breath, wondering about the child. Finally she hustled him off to the family doctor. "He's got too much energy; he never wears down," she sighed tiredly.

The doctor examined young Billy and said, "He's perfectly normal—it's just the way he's built." How prophetic that statement was, the years have since shown.

When Morrow put a broom in Billy Frank's hands, saying, "Here, sweep the porch," motioning to the big veranda which girdled the house, she was never quite certain what he'd do with the broom! She believed in teaching her children how to share in the home responsibilities.

Catherine and Billy were real buddies, riding their bicycles along dusty Park Road. They especially liked to play ball in the big front yard. When Morrow heard the sound of splintering glass, all she could think of was, "Oh, no! Not again."

When Billy was nine, the family moved from the white farmhouse to the big, two-story, red brick home which Mrs. Graham occupies to this day. On my visit she said, "I just love every plank and old nail in this house." Her desire is to live out her days in the lovely family home that has so many cherished memories.

The dairy herd which Frank had dreamed of having someday had become a reality. The house was roomy and rambling, and Frank had a little "office" off the living room with a metal desk and a phone.

Suburban Charlotte was spreading out, and the milk route Frank had established was growing. Morrow assisted with cow production records and helped her husband dispatch the monthly billings.

Morrow's day began when she stirred slightly as she heard her husband getting up early to do the chores and milk his cows. She would fall back asleep to arise later to prepare a hearty farmer's breakfast: plenty of milk, homemade bread, butter, hot cereal, fresh eggs, sausages or ham. When Melvin and Billy got to the right age when their father considered them ready, they likewise would arise at 2:30 to do their share of the farm work.

As the family gathered at the breakfast table, each member would bow his head and fold his hands as Frank Graham asked the blessing. After the meal he opened the family Bible and practiced memorizing Scripture with the children.

Morrow got up from the table and packed Billy's school lunch. As she moved about, she could hear her husband talking to Billy. The elder Graham would help as Billy repeated the verses he had been learning. "All right, recite," he would say, and Billy would repeat the particular psalm he was memorizing. A verse a day was expected. Billy today recalls those instructional periods as among the most important in his life, helping him to become saturated with the Bible. In preaching, he quotes from passages and verses he learned at the breakfast table.

Billy never did become known for studiousness in school. He boarded the school bus with as much enthusiasm as any of the other children, but his grades left something to be desired. Always the tallest boy in the class, he seemed to fall victim to every ambush and skirmish in Sharon Grammar School. At one time Billy was heard to say, "It appears that I spent an unseemly amount of time in school in combat."

If he wasn't learning much from the schoolbooks, he was having fun, making friends, and learning how to get along with people. He was very popular. Morrow described his reaction to girls like this: "Billy liked girls, and girls liked him. He would come to dinner many an evening, licking his lips and talking fast, saying, 'I met a new girl today, and she is about the cutest girl I ever saw in my whole life.' His cutest girls became a family joke!"

The children had happy times together. Melvin has recollections of watching Billy get on his bicycle and ride down Park Road; trailing along behind were his small black goat, his large brown goat, and the pet collie. Nothing pleased Billy more than if a car would happen along and everyone would turn to look at him and laugh! Morrow would stand at her living room window, watch the procession, and laugh too.

Billy Frank and Billy the goat were quite a team! Mr. Graham bought a beautiful wagon and, in Mrs. Graham's words, "the prettiest little harness." Off the Billies would go! Mrs. Graham continues,

"That goat would come to the back door, then would just stop until I'd throw a piece of bread, and then go on. But the goat wouldn't budge until he had that piece of bread. Sometimes Billy would have to call, 'Hey, Mom, throw out the bread.' " When the goat got tired of the whole thing, in the manner of stubborn goats he would just lie down and that was that! It was one problem Billy never could quite solve. Morrow cheerfully went along with this bit of goat-play and cooperated by saving her scraps of bread.

The Graham children counted among their best playmates and friends the children of Reese Brown and his wife. Reese was a tireless, efficient, and trustworthy Negro who taught the Graham boys to milk the herd. Racial pride was a stranger at the Graham home.

Morrow Graham never owned a book on child psychology, but she had the Bible. Today she says, "What would I have done without the Book of Proverbs?" When motherly instinct told her, "Spank," she remembered: "Foolishness is bound in the heart of a child; but the rod of correction shall drive it far from him" (Prov. 22:15), and she spanked.

When one of the children resisted discipline, she recalled: "The rod and reproof give wisdom: but a child left to himself bringeth his mother to shame" (Prov. 29:15), and out came the hickory switch.

When Billy Frank and his sisters and brothers balked at memorizing the Westminster Shorter Catechism—which seemed awfully long to them—Morrow Graham remembered: "Train up a child in the way he should go, And even when he is old he will not depart from it" (Prov. 22:6). And she saw to it that they memorized.

When her husband employed his belt for child correction, which wasn't too often, Morrow winced but recalled: "Withhold not correction from the child: for if thou beatest him with the rod, he shall not die" (Prov. 23:13). She might have wiped tears from her own eyes, turning her head so the children wouldn't see, but she knew her husband was doing what was biblically correct. The children didn't die! They were both reassured by Proverbs 13:24: "He that spareth his rod hateth his son: but he that loveth him chasteneth him betimes." It seems more than coincidence that the Book of Proverbs is one of Billy's favorite Bible sections today.

The warmth and comfort of an unselfish mother were accepted by the Graham children as their birthright. The Graham home was Scripture oriented with the family gathering in the den every evening to read the Bible. The children participated, reading verse by verse, taking turns. Then everyone would get down on his knees and participate in family prayers. "They prayed for their dogs, cats, everything—but they were learning to pray," recalls their mother.

Billy's brother Melvin says of those times, "I'll never forget our family devotions. It caused us to learn what we wouldn't have learned on our own."

In 1933 Morrow Graham's sister, Lil Barker, convinced Morrow she should take time out to attend a weekly Bible class. The result was revolutionary. "I couldn't wait to get back the next week! The class had something I desperately wanted more than anything, and, oh, I just couldn't wait," Mrs. Graham recalls. It was there that she came to understand that the Holy Spirit indwells a Christian's heart. "For six years I went to that class every week except two—I was so eager to learn," she declared.

In 1934 the Grahams lent a pasture to thirty local businessmen who wanted to devote a day to prayer for the city of Charlotte. These businessmen next erected a large "tabernacle" of raw pine in the city where the fiery Southern Baptist evangelist Mordecai Ham conducted meetings. His passionate preaching was to shake the complacency of churchgoing Charlotte.

At sister Lil's urging, Morrow and Frank attended the meetings. Fifteen-year-old Billy went also. His mother recalls it. "We saw Billy walk down that sawdust aisle and knew he was doing a wonderful thing; but my emotional experience about that came when we got home. Billy was in the breakfast room pretending to make a sandwich. He came and threw his arms around me and said, 'Mother, I'm a changed boy!' " Mrs. Graham paused in the conversation, wiped away a tear, and said, "It's hard to talk about it. . . ."

Melvin Graham, sitting nearby, commented, "I was ten or eleven when this happened, but I remember seeing Billy go forward. It really surprised me. The only thing I could remember him ever really wanting to do was to be a ball player. He talked about that a lot; he wanted to play for the Philadelphia Athletics. I remember sometime later when we were in the field plowing with the mules. We saw a little plane sky-writing. They were advertising something with the initials GPG. Billy immediately said, 'That means Go Preach the Gospel.' I looked at him and said, 'No, it doesn't. It means Go Plow the Ground!' "

Morrow Graham added, "Melvin was more interested in the dairy than Billy was. Billy would milk and help on the farm, but

73

Melvin put a lot more energy into it. I can look back now and see how the Lord was preparing Billy for what he is doing today."

Billy's best friend, Grady Wilson, had gone forward with Billy that night in the Ham revival meeting; and later Grady's older brother, T. W., made a similar public decision. The three continued their friendship through the years as they shared the work of the Billy Graham Evangelistic Association.

As Billy's high school graduation time approached, his home-room teacher stopped at the house one day and said, "Mrs. Graham, I'm so sorry to have to tell you this, but Billy is not going to make the grade."

Morrow stared at the teacher. She was stunned. "Oh, no, that can't be," she answered, her slim hands crossed on her chest fearfully. She knew Billy's grades were somewhat low, but surely not that bad.

"Yes, it is true. He's losing his strength, and his grades are very poor. Mrs. Graham, I think the boy is working too hard. He just can't do it—why, every morning at 11 o'clock he just falls asleep in class."

"I felt like I had just been chopped through the heart," Mrs. Graham confides. "I turned back into the living room and prayed, 'O Lord, that can't be true. You'll just have to do something for my boy.' Then the thought came—at Christmas time Billy had read ten or eleven historical books from the library, and so I remember finishing that prayer by saying, 'Lord, you are preparing him for this something, whatever it is. Lord, it's your problem.' You know, I left that problem with the Lord, and by the end of the school year, when he was seventeen, he had made the grades to graduate. It was surely a test for me as his mother, but God saw him through."

When it came time for Billy to go to college, the Grahams enrolled him at Bob Jones College in Cleveland, Tennessee. Grady Wilson was going, and Grady's brother, T. W., was already there. When they returned from leaving Billy at the school, Morrow turned to her husband and said, "Frank, honey, Billy has left the home fires, and he has been accustomed to opening the Word of God every day and praying; I believe that he will continue to do so. Even if he continues to read only a verse a day, I believe that God is going to use him. Let's have the faith to believe and ask God to continue to work in Billy's heart."

They agreed, and together they began a new prayer vigil. "Every day my husband and I would go up to our bedroom after lunch and get down on our knees and pray for Billy. We just felt it was necessary. We claimed that verse, 'Study to show thyself approved unto God, a workman that needeth not to be ashamed, rightly dividing the word of truth.' We prayed that prayer for him for seven years."

After half a year at Bob Jones College, Billy went to the Florida Bible Institute at Temple Terrace, near Tampa. Morrow remembers taking Billy there. "I thought it was the prettiest place I had ever seen—the most magnificent buildings. It had been a millionaire's resort estate. The grounds were gorgeous. I thought we couldn't leave Billy in a more beautiful spot, and you could just feel the wonderful Christian influence there."

Billy wrote home regularly twice a week. The letters told of his growing in spiritual concerns. "Mother," he wrote, "words can't express Florida Bible Institute. . . . I've never felt so close to God in my life. This is the first time I have really enjoyed studying the Word of God. . . . I love it here." When Billy sent her his picture from the institute inscribed, "To the dearest Mom in all the world to me," Morrow's heart was full to overflowing—surely God was answering their prayers.

At the institute Billy's friendship with the dean, John Minder, deepened. Opportunities for preaching arose, and Billy began practicing his sermons on squirrels and rabbits he could flag down on the golf course. During these years Billy experienced the heartache of a broken romance, but he could still write home to his parents, "I love him, the Lord Jesus, better every day."

Mrs. Graham had been praying that Billy could go on to college at Wheaton, Illinois, if it were the Lord's will. In 1940, when that became possible, no one could have been happier than Morrow Graham! But some things changed. "Up until this time," she says, "Billy had always written the most precious letters. They were full of affection and how the Lord was working in his life. Every little circumstance seemed to draw him closer to the Lord, and he used these circumstances and every experience to deepen his relationship to Christ. But when he went away to Wheaton, he was so busy studying and preaching that he didn't have time to write as many letters. I really missed them.

"But one letter he did write was very important, and I will never forget what he said. He wrote to tell us about meeting Ruth Bell, whom he later married, and he said, 'Mother, the reason I like Ruth so much is that she looks and reminds me of you.' I thought that was a compliment. Of course, Ruth is far above me," says the modest mother of Billy Graham.

Ruth Bell had many male admirers, but Billy was chief among

them! He brought her home that first summer after Wheaton to meet his parents. They loved her immediately, and when on August 13, 1943, she became Billy's bride, Morrow Graham could only thank the Lord for giving to her son someone who was so right for him.

Morrow made a personal policy to withhold her advice, both as a mother and mother-in-law, after her children were married. "My daughters-in-law are just precious to me, both Ruth, Billy's wife, and Peggy, Melvin's wife. We have devoted, affectionate love for each other," she says today.

The Grahams were following Ruth and Billy's marriage with concern and interest. When Billy became pastor of the Village Church in Western Springs, twenty miles southwest of Chicago, he became the speaker on the radio broadcast "Songs in the Night," a forty-five minute program of preaching and singing on one of Chicago's powerful stations at 10:15 on Sunday nights. Since Morrow and Frank Graham couldn't get the program on the house radio, they sat in their car and tuned that radio dial until they got the station loud and clear, then sat back marveling, "Is that really our Billy!"

The years have since recorded what Morrow Graham's elder son has done—Youth for Christ evangelistic rallies first in Chicago, later across the country, and still later in England; the years at Northwestern College in Minneapolis where he served as president while continuing evangelistic campaigns; and then his meteoric rise after the 1949 Los Angeles Crusade to become the world's best-known evangelist.

Frank and Morrow Graham traveled to various parts of the country to be with Billy at some of his major campaigns—later changed to "crusades." Morrow claimed Jeremiah 23:23 for Billy when he first went into Youth for Christ work. "Am I a God at hand, saith the Lord, and not a God afar off?" She was glad she had found that verse when she observed firsthand Billy's busy schedule, the throngs of people, and the stresses to which he was often subject. As a result of her confidence in the Lord's care, she has not feared for her son's life.

What has been the most heartwarming experience of the mother whose son is a counselor of presidents? There have been many, Morrow Graham admits; then she describes one. "Billy visited President Nixon's mother several times during her illness, and so when Mr. Nixon was in Charlotte campaigning, he said he wanted

76

to come out and see me and see what the farm was like. Yes, that was very special." She showed me a picture hanging on the wall in her bedroom showing President Nixon sitting beside her on the couch in her living room.

The living room, like the rest of the Graham home, reflects the fine taste of the delicate lady who presides there—the walls a beautiful blue-green hue, with furniture and accessories to enhance the feeling of warmth and charm. An open Bible lay on a table by the couch; near the fireplace were books authored by her famous son, and other fine works of literature. In the hall leading to the kitchen a bookcase was full of well-worn Christian books.

On a massive chest in the living room stands a picture of Billy Graham by the famous New York photographer Bachrach. Off the living room is a door leading to what was once the family den—where family prayers were wont to be made—now converted into a downstairs bedroom for Mrs. Graham.

The dining room is uncluttered—simple yet elegant in feeling. Off that is a separate breakfast room, and then a small but efficient kitchen. In one corner stands an old-fashioned cupboard that yielded snacks to the eager hands of Morrow's children.

In the backyard Morrow's German shepherd dog is creating a fuss. He wants in. "And then," says Mrs. Graham, "he wants out— out the front door so he can go off to the shopping center!"

The *Charlotte News* some years ago described the Graham homestead as being surrounded by large, old trees which Frank Graham himself set out thirty-five years ago. In those days the house was surrounded by gently rolling fields and pasture land. Today those fields have been taken over by Park Road Shopping Center, whose neon lights cast multicolored patterns over the arbor of muscadines that Billy planted as a youth. Some of the farm acreage has been turned into a large housing tract where, on the fringe of what was the Graham property, Morrow's daughter Catherine lives in her own home.

"Did you notice the ten-story office building as you drove into the yard?" Mrs. Graham asks. "Well, that is where the big dairy barn and two silos were. There are so many changes now, and it has come so quickly. My husband has been gone only seven and a half years." . . . Her voice trailed off into meaningful silence.

Mrs. Graham moves more slowly these days, the result of decalcification of bones in her left foot. Her once long blond hair has turned snowwhite, framing the fine features of her sweet face. The blue eyes, behind glasses, are kind and gentle, a sure reflection of the inner woman, a woman at peace with God. And why not? All four of her children love and serve the Lord they first learned about within the home.

How does she feel when she sees Billy on TV or attends a crusade? "I feel just real wonderful. And I just sit in awe . . . when I think of the great things the Lord has done."

Does she keep scrapbooks? "No, not any more. I did for years, but they became too heavy and large. I have five, but I had to quit."

How does she feel when Billy is misquoted or criticized? "It doesn't bother me, and it doesn't bother him either. The important thing is to be right in the eyes of God, and we know he is."

Her daughter Jean chimes in: "Mother always taught us, 'Be ye kindly affectionate one to another,' from the Bible, and 'Trust in the Lord in all thy ways.' Another verse that she told us over and over has really stuck with me: 'A word fitly spoken is like apples of gold in pictures of silver' (Prov. 25:11). These verses, and many others, explain Mother's reaction to things that affect Billy and all of us."

Does Billy get home very often? "Oh, yes, whenever he is in the area, he makes it a point to stop by. And he phones—he phones me regularly." She looked at Melvin and said, "Billy hasn't changed much, has he Melvin?"

Melvin replied, in the genial manner so much like his brother, "Nope, he sure hasn't. He's still the same old Billy."

Morrow Graham smiled. "When Billy was young, he liked to get down on the floor, right here," and she motioned to the spot in the living room. "He'd lie on his back, put his feet up, and read. You know, when he comes home now he takes off his coat, gets down on the floor the same way and reads—it may be the paper, his Bible or a book—but Billy hasn't changed. Just the other day he was home and did that, and I thought, 'Billy, you're just like you were when you were my twelve-year-old Billy Frank.' "

With her hands folded serenely in her lap, Morrow tilted her head to one side in a characteristic gesture and said, "The passage that has meant so much to me in the Bible is 2 Peter 1:3–9: 'According as his divine power hath given unto us all things that pertain unto life and godliness, through the knowledge of him that hath called us to glory and virtue: Whereby are given unto us exceeding great and precious promises; that by these ye might be partakers of the divine nature, having escaped the corruption that is in the world through lust. And besides this, giving all diligence, add to your faith virtue; and to virtue, knowledge; And to knowledge, temperance; and to temperance, patience; and to patience, godliness; And to godliness, brotherly kindness; and to brotherly kindness, charity. For if these things be in you, and abound, they make you that ye shall neither be barren nor unfruitful in the knowledge of our Lord Jesus Christ. But he that lacketh these things is blind, and cannot see afar off, and hath forgotten that he was purged from his old sins.' These verses have meant so much to me. As a young mother I had to learn patience, but the Lord dealt with me."

Yes, the Lord has dealt with her—and through her with untold thousands across the world. Though she may consider herself "just a little country woman," she had a godly vision of a mother's calling, and through such women the Lord accomplishes his purposes of bringing people to himself.

As she views the situation in the world today—campus unrest, turmoil between nations, rebellious youth, and the prevailing conditions throughout our land—Morrow Graham says: "I believe that if Deuteronomy 6:4–7 were practiced by parents, we would see far less unrest and problems in the country. The entire sixth chapter speaks to me of God-given home life and was most important in my life in bringing up our children."

And what does that passage say? "Hear . . . The Lord our God is one Lord: And thou shalt love the Lord thy God with all thine heart, and with all thy soul, and with all thy might. And these words, which I command thee this day, shall be in thine heart: And thou shalt teach them diligently unto thy children, and shalt talk of them when thou sittest in thine house, and when thou walkest by the way, and when thou liest down, and when thou risest up."

Morrow Graham's burden for the women of today is the same her son proclaims wherever he goes: that they will come to know Christ as their Savior, then get into Bible study and carry out its teachings in the daily experiences of life.

She prays unceasingly for her son, for her other children, for her twelve grandchildren, five great-grandchildren, and for worldwide needs.

When Billy Graham began his preaching ministry—back in his Florida Bible Institute days—he was heard to say, "The road to hell is blocked with many godly interferences . . . if you go to hell it will be your own deliberate choice, as God is doing his best to keep you out of there." Speaking on the theme of "God's Blockade," young Billy went on to explain, "Before a person can sink there, he must climb over the Bible, a mother's influence in prayer, the Holy Spirit, the mountain of reason, and the Cross of Christ. . . ."

*A mother's influence in prayer*—these words stand out as one contemplates the life of Morrow Graham. In her shy, unassuming way she comments: "We try—as mothers we try. Yet, there is so much of weakness and failure in our own lives, we just wonder how God overlooks all of this and brings good out of evil. We had such long hours and hard work, but we surely did read the Bible and pray."

That made so many differences. . . . Morrow Graham would never admit being a great mother behind a great son, but she does confirm she has a great God, one who lavishes blessings unto children's children.

# *Josephine Johnson*

## mother of WALLACE JOHNSON

He came into the house, threw down his cap dejectedly, and said, "Mother, I want to go to Georgia Tech."

His mother looked up from her work and calmly replied, "Wallace, you know you can't."

"Yes, I can . . . I just know you and Dad could send me, there'd be some way."

Quietly, in her altogether reasonable way which he knew so well, Wallace E. Johnson's mother answered, "Wallace, you can't go to college until you finish high school."

"I can't! I can't do that!" and he flew off to his bedroom.

Wisely, she left him alone and went on with dinner preparations, taking time to make something she knew her son liked especially well. "Come along, Wallace, hop up, I've got something special for dinner." Not one word was said about high school and the previous conversation.

For one week high school dropout Wallace Johnson went about his work as a builder with a troubled mind. At age sixteen he had become a full-fledged carpenter, learning how to read a scale, how to estimate and make blueprints—all that was involved in the building trade. When he was eighteen, he lacked two years before finishing high school, but dollars were more important than a diploma. He already had $1,800 in the bank. A contract came his way to build a house in Moorhead, Mississippi. It took him two years to complete that project. By the time he put together the jigsaw puzzle parts of an imported French mantelpiece, the house had cost $11,000. His $1,800 was gone and he was $400 in debt.

"I was broke," he reminisces, "just as broke as I could be." Sensing that he needed to round out his education, he approached his mother. Her suggestion that he go back to high school was met with open rebellion. "That was a bitter pill. I was almost as tall as I am now," said the six-foot, three-inch Johnson. "Going broke was bad enough, but then to have mother suggest I go back to high school when I was already twenty years old.". . .

One week later, he put his arms around her and said, "Mother, I want you to know I'm going to take your advice to finish school."

We were sitting in the handsomely appointed office of Wallace E. Johnson, vice chairman of Holiday Inns, Inc., wide-ranging entrepreneur and builder, dedicated Christian layman. Graciously he had received me on short notice, shoving aside his extremely busy schedule to accommodate an interview while I was in Memphis for a few hours.

Later, I sat in Mrs. Johnson's room at Rosewood Convalescent Center in Memphis and interviewed her.

Her undaunted enthusiasm and faith in her son's ability kept him going twenty-four months of school. During that time she urged him, "Wallace, take all the speech courses you can get—learn how to compose yourself, how to get up and make a delivery. If you don't learn to speak your mind, your eyes and hands will be speaking for you the rest of your life." Trying to conceal her rightful pride, Mrs. Johnson said, "I kind of think that helps him today, don't you?" No one would argue with that. When Wallace Johnson travels and speaks across the country, or when he addresses his business constituents on any of the seventy-eight corporations he heads or in which he holds office, no doubt can be in anyone's mind that here is a man who knows how to express himself very well!

Wallace Johnson graduated from high school in 1923 at age twenty-two. He never did go on to college. A position was offered to him to manage a retail lumberyard, and he gave it everything he had. Today he refers to himself as "Mississippi's No. 1 dropout" and "a poor little old peckerwood boy from Mississippi"; yet his is one of the most remarkable success stories in the annals of American business.

When Gordon College presented him with the honorary Doctor of Laws degree for his outstanding contributions to many Christian and humanitarian causes, Wallace Johnson was thinking of his mother whose encouragement and faith in him had been demonstrated—not forced—and had put him on the right road to real learning many years before.

Of herself Mrs. Johnson says, "The great men in my life are in answer to prayer. I married a Christian boy; the very first meal we had together he returned thanks, and every night before we would retire, we would read a chapter in his little red Testament which I still have."

Her eyes sparkled, even at the age of ninety-one, as she recalled her spirited approach to marriage. The dimples in her cheeks and chin still showed, though the years have left some "lines of living" as she shared, "My husband called my dimples 'his kiss box.' "

Her marriage to Felix Alva Johnson lasted fifty glorious years. Two days before he died, they were holding hands, recalling their wonderful years as man and wife.

Her advice to wives was summed up in a practical old-fashioned but beautiful philosophy: "Darn John's socks, straighten those cuffs on his suit, sew that button on—do it all with kindness, a little extra patience, and plenty of love. And when confronted with a problem, take it—but take it to the Lord—in prayer, and it will surprise you what he will do!"

Such an attitude is not surprising from one who has walked close to God all her life and therein found her Reason for living and her Source of strength to meet every situation. At the time of my visit she could say, "I've been a Christian for eighty years."

As a child of eleven she had gone to a revival service and sensed she ought to give her heart to God. When she and her sisters arrived home, one sister said, "Mother, Jo's under conviction." The mother grabbed her little daughter's hand and took her into the bedroom where they knelt down. At age ninety-one she could remember with clarity that moment. "After just a little bit of talk it seemed like all my sins rolled away and I had a Savior."

This same deep faith found expression throughout her marriage. At the birth of Wallace she and her husband recognized that they couldn't raise their baby without the Lord's help.

Did Wallace require much discipline in his growing-up years? No, he was an obedient child and did not require a great amount of stern discipline. Her philosophy on child rearing didn't come from books or lectures, but was the result of a prayerful approach to her God-given responsibility of being a mother. Even before Wallace was born, she prayed, "God, give me what I can mother the best." God answered that prayer by instilling into her practical precepts which she used in lovingly ministering as a mother.

Family devotions were a regular practice as was attendance at Sunday school. In rainy and inclement weather Mrs. Johnson would have her husband round up the neighborhood children and give them Sunday school in the home, reading to them from *Hurlbut's Story of the Bible*.

It may have been her husband who gave their son his love for building. "One Christmas he gave him a little box of toy carpenter tools—saw, hammer, square, chisel, and a little box of nails. So Wallace learned to handle the tools of carpentry when he was quite young.

"When he was just a little fellow and I made him his everyday pants, he wanted a pocket in the back. Then he'd want a long envelope and he'd put it there. He was sticking a pencil behind his ear by the time he was two years old! As he got older, he was always asking for a nickel so he could buy some nails, and my husband would provide some lumber. Many a time they would go to the store together and buy Wallace a handful of nails.

"When Wallace was sixteen a man asked him if he could build a chicken house. Wallace built it perfectly. Then he built some other smaller coops. That was his introduction to the carpenter trade." Wallace Johnson's building enterprises today extend from homes to multi million dollar hospitals.

Early in life Mrs. Johnson encouraged her son to choose his friends carefully. "Seek the best company or go alone, but treat everybody right," were her words of admonition. When he walked down the aisle at age eleven in their little community church to receive Christ as his personal Savior, there was no overt coaxing, pressure, or urging from his parents or outsiders. It was the result of consistent home training, giving of the Word, of Bible study, faithful church and Sunday school attendance, and prayers.

"The most important thing mothers can do for their children is to love them and tell them the truth. A mother's tongue should not be like a whip. Keep on praying 'til you pray things through. God's great promises are always true. Maybe his answers won't be what we expect, but God's ways are better than ours."

The years have etched themselves into the happy face of Mrs. Josephine Johnson. As she talks her countenance is flooded with a look of peace and contentment that can only come from having lived secure in the knowledge that what has come to her has come from the hand of God. She speaks from a wealth of personal experience, not just theory.

What was her definition for happiness? "Happiness is practice— let the sunshine in, keep on the sunnyside." Her quick mind responded to such questions with bright little sayings which evidenced her own lifelong sunny disposition.

Smiling, she mused, "Be still, sad heart, and cease your pining, for behind the cloud the sun is still shining. Yes, even on the day your loved one is taken from you, recognize that in everything God has a purpose and he has a plan, and it will be better than the one you were working on."

What was her first indication that her son might be different, and to what did she attribute his success? "I always told Wallace to first be good, then be smart. When Wallace listened to this and put it into practice, I knew he'd be all right. The secret of his success can be attributed to his praying and trusting in the Lord continually. You have to pray without ceasing."

Wallace Johnson learned that "secret" at his mother's knee. Of her he says, "Mother's devoted Christian life has been an inspiration to me every hour of my life. She is possessed with the radiant happiness of being a Christian and is daily devoted to prayer."

With serene confidence born out of long years in such communion with her Lord, the sweet-faced, white-haired precious little queen-lady of Rosewood Convalescent Center folded her tiny wrinkled hands, and in that charming southern way, observed, "There are too many mothers and fathers today who are supposed to be heads of homes without really being what they ought to be.

85

Young mothers today are letting their children raise them. You mothers get back on your knees, read your Bibles, and start putting into practice what you're reading. If you do this, God will see and answer your prayers."

Mrs. Johnson has always possessed the gift of artistry, and her work is displayed throughout the nursing home where she lives, in addition to a special room in the offices of the Holiday Inns and in her son's private offices. Her sensitive spirit shows in these paintings and in the other creative things she still does. In 1969 she had painted seven pictures, sewn by hand twelve aprons, and planted a garden beneath her window that had produced two hundred cucumbers from two vines (all of which she had the fun of giving away), and lovingly tended and watched grow a variety of roses.

Many things have been written about Wallace Johnson, but much less has been said about the little praying mother behind him. Yet, he would be the first to tell you she has been a great influence behind his life.

# Alma Johnson

### wife of WALLACE JOHNSON

The final chapter of the book of Proverbs declares the praise and properties of a good wife, a virtuous woman. Among other things we read: "Who can find a virtuous woman? for her price is far above rubies. The heart of her husband doth safely trust in her, so that he shall have no need of spoil. She will do him good and not evil all the days of her life. . . . She considereth a field, and buyeth it."

Alma Johnson, wife of Wallace E. Johnson, multimillionaire builder, fits that description. Together she and her husband have worked side by side through the years, beginning with the home building industry, moving on to the co-founding of Holiday Inns, Inc., starting a chain of extended care facilities known as Medi-centers of America, Inc., and presently serving on the boards of seventy-eight corporations. But their business accomplishments are only a part of the picture, for theirs is a story of a partnership in prayer that has had a far-reaching impact which cannot be chronicled.

Ask Wallace Johnson what has been most helpful to him in his career and he'll unhesitatingly tell you, "My wife. I have the greatest wife a man ever had. She is the dearest, solidest Christian you can find. She is really a powerhouse of a thinker. She is an officer in most of our enterprises and always available for consultations, helping to make decision after decision. She has this terrific business sense; not only does she think through these tremendously important matters, but she has this remarkable 'feel' for particular things."

To understand and appreciate why this successful man should credit his wife with contributing so greatly to his success, an interview was arranged with "Mrs. Alma," as he affectionately calls her. Here then is her story.

"Wallace and I met in the sixth grade. At that time we hardly knew each other—I was more the age of his younger brother and ran around with that group. After a while, however, we started going together, although we both dated others. Before long I started comparing him with other fellows, and they just didn't measure up to him! I guess it was his personality. He was a perfect gentleman, the type of person everyone immediately liked. And he was a good salesman!" She laughed at that; the implication was clear.

Of their meeting Wallace Johnson says, "She was as pretty as a speckled pup on a banana wagon."

After four years of going together, Alma McCool and Wallace Johnson became man and wife on August 10, 1924. Wallace borrowed $85 for the occasion. "I got married on a Sunday at ten o'clock," he recalls, "and at two o'clock I went to the lumberyard and fed the mules. I went to work the next morning at the lumberyard, but we've had just one big, long honeymoon all these years." He had finished high school and was manager of a retail lumber yard in Itta Bena, Mississippi, earning $125 a month.

Their first home was a rented bungalow on a lakefront street which Alma described as "a very romantic spot." From the start of their married life Wallace proved to be very ambitious and worked hard. "I had to learn patience—many a night I would sit with a prepared dinner, warming it over and over again, thinking he'd be home any moment. Hours didn't mean a thing to him. Then I began to realize it was as much my job as his to help him achieve success. My part was to look after him and our home, to be cheerful and sympathetic, to create a happy atmosphere. We lived as well as anyone else but were always struggling to do better—looking forward to better days. We made sacrifices but didn't mind it. We agreed on goals and worked together toward that end."

Alma had been reared in a Christian home. She and her one brother were surrounded with love. It was a very closely knit family. As a young girl she realized the claims of Christ and has never veered from a life of faith and commitment. Of his wife's convictions Mr. Johnson says, "My wife is not only a brilliant executive secretary who knows as much about my business as I do, she is also a spiritual partner. Every day we read Scripture together and pray about our mutual concerns. We've had some real problems—opportunities—but we have always been able to pray them through together. When things aren't happening right, Alma will say, 'Wallace, you just haven't prayed about it enough.' "

They had been married five years when the depression hit. That was also the year their little girl was born. She died as an infant soon thereafter. That was a deep disappointment. "After waiting all those years for a child, it was hard to understand," she says with a faraway look in her eyes, but then she smiles and goes on, "but we knew there was a purpose in it. Now I feel that purpose may have been that I would never have become involved in business with my husband—you can't spend as much time with business as I have and raise a family."

Though the Johnsons lost their only child, through their humanitarian efforts they now have many children.

Wallace was determined to learn everything he could about the lumber business. When an opportunity came his way to go with a saw mill firm in Pine Bluff, Arkansas, that would teach him the manufacturing end of the business, he wanted to make the change, explaining that he already understood the retail side. Again their faith was put to the test when abruptly he lost that job.

Of that experience Wallace Johnson states: "That closed door in Pine Bluff was just as much an indication of God's will for my life as every open door I have experienced. In fact, I feel indebted to the man who fired me."

Her faith unwavering, Alma stood by. "Our plans are often shifted by circumstances. God had his reasons." Future days were to prove this true in ways they could not possibly have foreseen.

Wallace decided to run a blind ad in a Memphis newspaper, describing himself and his qualifications. FHA was just getting started and a former employer of Wallace saw the ad, thought he recognized that it might be Wallace Johnson, and sent him a letter stating: "If this is Wallace Johnson who worked for me previously, report for duty Monday morning."

It was spring, and that letter sent them to Memphis to see about the job, Alma wearing a smart gray suit and carrying a black patent purse. In that purse was their last twenty dollars, every dollar in the world that they had.

They stayed at the Chisca Hotel. The next morning Wallace said, "Alma, do you have the purse?" and she answered, "No, you have it." They turned the room upside down and couldn't find the purse.

Wallace panicked. Not waiting for the elevator, he rushed down the stairs. "I turned that car inside out and still couldn't find the purse. Just fifteen cents was all I had in my pocket."

Soon Alma joined him. It was a two-door car in which you had to turn the seats down. When Wallace turned one of the seats down, the purse fell right at Alma's feet. She picked it up; they got into the car and drove all the way down Union Avenue without saying a word to each other. They were so relieved they were speechless. Wallace took the job, and Alma has not owned a black patent purse since then!

It was 1939 and Wallace Johnson had been working as a $37.50 salesman for a building supply firm when he approached his wife about the wisdom of going into business for himself. "Alma, I'm frustrated and discouraged. Nothing seems to be going right."

It was a turning point. Faithful in church attendance, believing in God, yet Wallace had disassociated his job from his faith. As they prayed, Wallace became very specific: "Lord, I've been trying to make a go of it as a salesman, but I'm not doing very well. What am I doing wrong? Show me, Lord, the direction I should go, the people I should see, the way I should use my time."

From that moment on, things began to fall into place. Trying to accomplish everything on his own resources had resulted in disappointment. Praying for guidance made a difference. Names of people to see, places to go popped into his mind. "Alma, these suggestions can only come from God!" He was excited. His mind became flooded with ideas. Alma's excitement matched her husband's.

A new law permitted the Federal Housing Authority to insure 90 percent on the loan of a home. This was a radical, and much needed, departure for home building. Previously, lenders would loan only 60 percent. "Alma, let's borrow on our car and go into the home building business."

With a $250 loan secured against his old secondhand Ford they began. Wallace Johnson was thirty-nine years old, and the future looked promising as he set out to build a five-room house for $3,000. He made it with a dollar to spare and sold it at a $300 profit. That year, Johnson built 80 more homes and the following year built 365.

Her husband was asked to speak at a home show to a group of manufacturers, and Alma went along. Some of the salesmen were standing around talking and laughing about what a Johnson built home must look like for that price. Not knowing that she was Wallace Johnson's wife, they continued their discussion. She took it as long as she could and then, rising to her feet, said, "Gentlemen, I'd like to say a few words. The houses you are talking about have five rooms beautifully color-coordinated. They have tile, good floors, plenty of closet and cupboard space, screened porches, and one bathroom. In other words, they are very nice homes." Then, turning to one especially vocal man, she addressed her words, "And if the roof isn't any good, it's your fault, they are your shingles." Turning slightly, she looked at another critic and commented, "And if the paint job is bad, it's your fault, for we use your paint." It was the perfect squelch and had a tremendous effect.

There were more than fifteen thousand lots for sale scattered all over Memphis, with curbs, gutters, utilities, sidewalks—and weeds and grass. Wallace Johnson didn't own a single lot, but he was imaginative. "Alma, let's make some signs. We can help people sell these lots."

Soon four hundred to five hundred signs were appearing on lots all over the city reading: "Let Wallace E. Johnson build your home on this lot." The phone number of their home was given. Alma recalls, "People began calling. I became the secretary, the superintendent on the job, and did the sketching, too. Wallace was busy building. We couldn't really afford it, but I would buy *House Beautiful, Home and Garden,* and all the magazines I could find. Then I'd read all about interior decorating and look at floor plans. When

91

people would call indicating an interest in a certain lot, we'd buy the lot from the owner and sell it to the interested party, let him choose a sketch, and before we knew what was happening, we were building houses from one end of town to the other."

Front page newspaper headlines stated: "Wallace E. Johnson Starts 10 Houses." Then it was an unheard of thing for someone to build that many houses at one time. Things progressed at such a pace that soon they were building the first low-rental housing projects in the southern part of the country. Since they couldn't afford to hire anyone to manage the business aspects, Alma did the banking, the buying of materials, the bargaining and promoting. "I would make inspections every day. I knew every man on the job, all by their first names. We had both black and white men working at the going rate of 25¢ an hour for common labor. I had never thought I would be interested in business, but it was fascinating. Wallace and I began to feel we were really accomplishing something for humanity. At that time many couples couldn't even rent an apartment, and they were living with one of the parents. Many times we saw couples on the verge of separation because of friction caused by living conditions. They were able to qualify for FHA loans and buy our homes. We took a personal interest in these people, and later it was just wonderful to drive by, see the little children out playing on the lawn and the happy expressions on the people's faces."

In 1942 they started, finished, and sold one thousand houses. By 1945 that number had tripled. When the war came along, all of the painters were drafted except one man. In near panic Wallace said, "Alma, I don't see how we can build anymore—the banks will foreclose. We can't finish up these homes without painters."

"Give me time to think, Wallace," was her reply. Soon she came back to him. "Women are doing everything else these days; let's teach women how to paint." They had one man painter left who hadn't been drafted. He was drafted to train women painters!

Wallace said, "Go to town and buy whatever you need in the way of coveralls. I'll put an ad in the paper: 'Wanted, women to paint houses.' We'll get those houses finished yet!"

In the next few days, they had a hundred women learning how to paint. They had paint on their eyebrows, in their hair, and all over themselves. But at one point through those years there were three hundred women on the weekly payroll doing nothing but painting. Alma's quick thinking had saved the day.

During the war when homes were being built, the builder was

allowed to sell only 25 percent of them and had to keep the rest for rentals. At the end of the war the Johnsons owned 325 rental homes in Memphis. A business associate pessimistically said, "You'll never get your money out of those houses." But Alma viewed the scene in quite a different way.

"There were marriages going on all the time. The boys in service would need homes when they got out. I had a feeling we wouldn't have enough homes to sell." Her feelings once again proved true.

The demand for housing was great. Firmly believing that the home is more than just a physical shelter, that it is the spiritual center of our culture, the Johnsons asked for guidance to construct two thousand homes in 1945. It seemed like a fantastic goal! They wondered where the money would come from. Yet, they dared to believe, and at year's end they had actually built three thousand homes.

The war was over. Now they were free to sell the rentals. Replacement prices on homes were going up; in fact, the whole economy of the nation was spiraling. The servicemen were, indeed, coming home, getting married, qualifying for FHA loans, getting good jobs, needing places to live. One day Alma called her husband and their banker and said, "Let's go for a ride. I want to look at some of our building projects."

Wallace Johnson had three thousand houses on his hands and in quiet desperation was letting his salesmen sell the equity in the houses for $300 or $400. Alma was aware of this and it bothered her sixth sense.

As they drove along she pointed, "What are we selling that house for?" and Wallace glanced at the list in his lap and would tell her. Her answer: "Raise that one a thousand dollars." They kept on driving and everywhere they went she asked the same question. When Wallace would answer, "That one is selling for $3,000," she would say, "Raise it to $4,000." In four hours of driving and looking, she had raised the price of housing in Memphis by a million dollars.

As she describes it, "Wallace about went to pieces, and he kept saying, 'Sweetheart, you're fixin' to ruin us!'"

In the back seat the banker was having an even worse time than Wallace Johnson! Yet, the houses continued to sell.

Several weeks later she had them accompany her on the same drive and suggested the same thing, raising another million dollars just like that!

They began making a daily list of things to pray about. Sometimes on note paper, sometimes on the back of an old envelope, they'd jot down their prayer concerns. The business continued to prosper, and with it they began tithing their time and money to churches and charitable causes.

The next big step for the Johnsons came when they envisioned the need for motels across the nation. This dream had its beginning when they tried to find comfortable lodging for themselves in a community where they were doing some building. Wallace suffered from hay fever and allergies and spent sleepless nights walking on the dirty rugs in the musty old hotels. When they finished the building project, Alma's brother approached them and said, "We need to put a motel out there on the highway." Wallace agreed and said, "Barney, you design it, and, Alma, you take care of furnishing it." Soon a thirty-two-room motel had risen on the spot.

One day a very good builder friend, Kemmons Wilson, was visiting with the Johnsons, and Wallace said, "Kemmons, you should go into the motel business. I'll give you the plans we used for our motel." Kemmons took the plans and expressed an interest in the idea. Shortly after that the Wilson family (five children) went on a vacation and came back very discouraged. "Wallace and Alma, do you know it's almost impossible to take a family on a vacation? It just costs too much; they charge for each child! Not only that, but the rooms are small, the beds are narrow, there aren't any swimming pools, and it's just not fun!" Kemmons then went to work to build the first Holiday Inn in Memphis that would incorporate all of these extras no one had seen fit to give the traveling public to that date. The year was 1952.

Early in 1953 Kemmons came over to visit with the Johnsons again, and Kemmons said, "How about working together to make Holiday Inns into a nationwide venture?" The Johnsons agreed it was a great idea. That night they hammered out the plans for this new system until two o'clock in the morning.

Mr. Johnson was active in the National Association of Home Builders, and so he sent seventy-five letters of invitation to builders all over the nation inviting them to come to Memphis. Alma fixed a dinner and sixty-five showed up. The motel business had a questionable reputation at that time. The businessmen were excited about the possibilities of the venture, but not convinced. Three of them bought franchises.

Success came, but it did not happen overnight. It took patience. Work. Patience. Work. And faith!

Alma would not accept temporary failure as defeat. Her brother was traveling across the country in the Johnson station wagon selling the franchises. He believed in the idea also, but needed money. Wallace had put up several hundred thousand dollars, as had Kemmons, but the past record of the motel business was hard to overcome. Mortgage money was hard to get on a business that had no past history to its credit. One day Wallace told Alma that they had put up all the money he thought they should. Alma looked him in the eye and said, "I think you're making a mistake."

At that very time her brother came to her and said, "Alma, I just know you have some money somewhere to spare. We just have to travel on and sell these franchises. I know we can do it." It was the one time Wallace Johnson's wife did not consult her husband. Her brother had assured her the sale of the franchises was catching momentum, and they were at a turning point. She advanced a few thousand dollars.

Sometime later after the success of the new company was evident, she confessed to Kemmons and Wallace about her secret account and how the moneys were used to help make Holiday Inns a successful venture. Her faith in the concept of the idea has remained fixed. Today there are more than 1,382 Holiday Inns—a room is finished every twenty-two minutes, with a new Inn opening every two and one-half days. Kemmons Wilson, the original founder of Holiday Inns, remains as board chairman; and Wallace Johnson has been president until recently when he moved up to become vice chairman, which position has freed him from some of the myriad detail involved with the enterprise.

The Inns succeeded because the venture was timed right. People were traveling, taking vacations, wanting comfortable places to stay. Once again, the Johnsons, sensing a need, moved in.

The Inns have a policy of the open Bible in each room. There are many testimonies that have come as a result of this in the past —letters thanking them for the open Bible, letters sharing how people have been helped as a result of picking up the Bible and reading it. The one letter that most graphically describes what can happen as a result of this came from a man who stayed in the Birmingham, Alabama, Holiday Inn. When he left his home that morning he carried a gun, intending to commit suicide. His daughter lacked two months of finishing college, and he was faced with financial ruin. At this Inn, as he prepared to shoot himself, his eyes fell upon the open Bible. He reached for it and began to read. Then he got down

95

on his knees and prayed to God for help. He wrote to say that seeing the open Bible had saved his life.

Holiday Inns, Inc., is a publicly owned corporation. The Johnsons are sometimes criticized because in the Inn restaurants liquor is sold. Mr. Johnson explains: "When the issue of liquor comes up, I always vote against it. In the case of franchise holders, they, of course, control the matter in their Inns. I do not drink. I do not serve intoxicating beverages at meetings which I host. My vote is one vote, and I am out-voted."

In 1953 when Alma received word that her father, Mr. Ernest McCool, was very ill and needed institutional care, she had no choice but to place him in a general hospital. This showed the Johnsons the need for building convalescent centers for others having ailments similar to Alma's father.

The first such convalescent center was built in 1961 in Memphis. Eleven more have opened since then. Alma's father did not live long enough to enter one of these centers, but Mr. Johnson's mother now lives at Rosewood Convalescent Center in Memphis.

These centers were the forerunner of a new concept Kemmons Wilson and Wallace Johnson are developing with Medicenters of America, Inc., another in a growing number of far-flung interests and enterprises of this southern dynamo and his equally dynamic wife.

Alma Johnson's philosophy is straightforward and uncomplicated. "When Mr. Johnson gets frustrated, I just say, 'Now, Wallace, you just forgot to put that on your prayer list.'

"You can't just say, 'Lord, solve this problem,' and go about with a do-nothing attitude. You can't ask God for a hundred dollars and sit down and expect him to provide it. We are supposed to be intelligent people, and God intends for us to use what he has given to us in the way of wisdom. If we pray and rely on God's guidance, he will provide the wisdom in every area of our lives. Then it's up to us to do our part and work for him.

"I have always prayed that the Lord would give us wisdom in all our business and that we would make a reasonable profit. But in the next breath I would say that we will spend that profit wisely, that we would use this wisdom that he has given to us to help our fellow-man, to do what we can to make this world a better place in which to live."

The Wallace E. and Alma E. Johnson Foundation, a nonprofit corporation, was established in 1944. The foundation helps churches, hospitals, and sends young men through college to be ministers and doctors. Their philanthropies are vast, but Wallace and Alma have a belief that "when you do good, you should just shut up about it . . . it's between you and God."

Wallace Johnson does like to talk about his wife, however, and is proud to say, "I have the sweetest wife in the world. I have never closed a telephone conversation with her without saying, 'I love you.' I guarantee you we're happy!"

Alma, in turn, goes to the door every morning when her husband leaves for work, kisses him good-bye, and then says, "Wallace, I love you; I'll be praying for you."

This is the pattern that has gone on throughout their married life. I believe it is one that God honors. Yes, Alma Johnson has done her husband good all the days of her life, even as the writer of Proverbs has described.

# Evelyn LeTourneau

## wife of R. G. LeTOURNEAU

She strode into the meat market, walked up to the showcase, and when the man behind the counter said, "Good morning, what can I do for you today?" she answered nonchalantly, "I need two thousand pounds of hamburger."

"All right," the man answered, sliding the meat case door open. He reached in for the hamburger, and suddenly it hit him. *"Two thousand pounds . . . did you say two thousand pounds?"*

The straight face she'd been managing to hold could no longer keep from smiling. Evelyn LeTourneau laughed while the meat market man's eyes opened wide in disbelief and his jaw dropped open.

Assuring the man she really needed it, Evelyn went on into the grocery store and proceeded to astonish still more clerks with her list of 250 pounds of corn meal, six 100-pound sacks of onions, and forty-two cases #2 size cans of tomatoes. Then she went home, sat down and wrote a letter to her sister in California, asking her to send six hundred cans Grandma's Brand chili powder.

If R. G. LeTourneau wanted his favorite hot tamale pie to serve eight thousand people, his wife was determined to see that he had his wish fulfilled. That was in 1942.

R. G. LeTourneau and his family had moved to Vicksburg, Mississippi, where his third plant was opening and a big dedication service was planned. That's when he told his wife he wanted her to serve his favorite dish. Evelyn gasped when he confronted her with this request. "But R. G.," she sputtered, "I know how to cook that for eight people, but eight thousand!"

Undaunted R. G. had replied, "Evelyn, can't you just take the ingredients for eight and multiply them by a thousand? And don't worry about what you'll cook it in, I'll take care of that."

And he did! For a man who was a genius in the field of earth-moving machinery, providing a kettle large enough to cook hot tamale pie for eight thousand people was a comparatively easy task! R. G. had a huge piece of steel brought into the plant, rolled it up on the ends, welded it, set it down in a framework, lifted it up from the bottom off the concrete, installed gas tubing under the entire "kettle" and ignited a fire. The "kettle" was five feet wide, four feet deep, and twenty feet long.

Evelyn went to the hardware store, bought eight new garden hoes, put four boys on either side of the "kettle" standing on a bench, and they kept the mixture stirred all the while it was cooking. When it was ready R. G. provided a big crane which lifted the "kettle" and set it into another framework with wheels. It was a simple matter to wheel the "kettle" down the aisle and within forty minutes the eight thousand people were eating Evelyn's famous hot tamale pie, R. G.'s favorite!

The meat market man stood to one side, rubbed his eyes in disbelief—there was a ton of hamburger in that "kettle." Who but R. G. LeTourneau would have thought of doing that? And who but his wife, ever equal to his wild dreams, would have dared tackle such an undertaking?

Evelyn LeTourneau says, "That was the biggest thing I ever tackled for him. R. G. just thought there wasn't anything I couldn't do if I wanted to." But Evelyn LeTourneau has proved herself countless times in varied ways as a devoted wife, mother, friend, and counselor. Her life with R. G. LeTourneau had its beginning August 29, 1917.

The first time R. G. LeTourneau laid eyes on Evelyn she was a twelve-year-old in high-button shoes, gingham dress, and two huge ribbons tied to long, blonde braids. He was twelve years her senior and found her questions as intriguing as her looks. "If you broke your neck, why aren't you dead?"

He looked at this mischievous imp trying to decide on an appropriate answer, but before he could reply she asked another question. "When your head tilts over like that, do you see things sideways or like I do?" Was she only twelve? Now it was he who was asking the questions! To himself of course!

At that time R. G. was a mechanic. A high-bodied stock car he was testing slammed against the auto track rails. Later he was to claim that not only had this broken his neck, but it contributed to his becoming bald at an early age!

Oscar Peterson, Evelyn's father, was a second generation Swede who had a moving van and general draying business in Stockton, California. Mr. Peterson and Bob LeTourneau became friends, and when the Petersons invited him to move in and board with them, he accepted the invitation. Later, after being bombarded with questions by Evelyn and her younger brothers and sister, he wondered why he had made such a move!

As for Evelyn, life took on a different shade of meaning when Bob LeTourneau entered the picture. While she unabashedly had peppered him with questions on their first meeting, now she suddenly began to find herself tongue-tied in his presence and would run to her room and pray, "God, oh God, please have him wait for me."

When Bob LeTourneau's parents moved to Stockton, Bob moved in with them, but he seemed to be spending a lot of evenings at the Petersons. The Evelyn he had met in high-buttoned shoes was now wearing pumps. The gingham dress had been discarded in favor of a silk dress for special occasions, and he considered her "something to behold." Road-testing the cars he had repaired during the day became an evening venture with Evelyn at his side.

The two of them came to an "understanding," and it was mutual love. There was one hitch to their relationship—Oscar Peterson, the stubborn Swede, told Bob LeTourneau he could marry his daughter but he'd have to wait five years until she came of age.

To Evelyn and Bob five years looked like a hundred. Love would find a way and they did! They eloped with Evelyn lacking several months of her seventeenth birthday.

They headed down the California coast toward Mexico. Evelyn hadn't been able to grab a coat, and the chill air nearly paralyzed her with its cold. Bob stopped at an all-night garage and picked up a bargain in lap robes, threw them around his child-bride, and drove like crazy. He knew Oscar Peterson would have alerted the authorities. He had!

Along the way he picked up hitchhikers. If the law was looking for an eloping couple, they wouldn't have chosen to investigate the Saxon roadster with the hitchhiking sheepherder and his dog, two migrant fruit pickers, and a dust-coated young girl. It was most unromantic.

They were married in Tijuana, turned right around and drove all the way back to Stockton. Bob LeTourneau was anxious to get things straightened out with the Petersons. Their beginning may have been inauspicious, but later, after 52 years of married life they could look back and declare they'd have done it again. Their love only grew with time.

They set up housekeeping in a single room with a gas hotplate to cook on. World War I was on, and R. G. went to work for the Mare Island Navy Yard. Evelyn solved their housing problem by moving to an old farmhouse fifteen miles up in the hills. She had to pump her own water, clean the kerosene lamp chimney, fight packrats, raise her own vegetables, but it was better than the single room.

By late summer of 1918 it was apparent that she couldn't live out there with R. G. coming home so seldom. They were about to make their parents grandparents, and so she moved into Stockton with friends. One night she received a phone call informing her that her husband was not expected to live through the night. The great Spanish influenza epidemic was sweeping across the country, killing people by the thousands, and it had felled her husband.

A few nights later, Caleb, their first son was born. Evelyn received a phone call again saying her husband was a bit better and they held out some hope that he would live. The baby was ten days old before R. G. was able to get out of the hospital. On February 9, 1919, their infant son died. It was a crisis time in their lives.

Numb with sorrow and shock, Evelyn and R. G. faced reality and the Lord. They acknowledged that they had not been living for him. Upon returning to Stockton to live, after their son's birth, R. G. had gone into the garage business again. As they reviewed their past, they knew the emphases in their marriage had been on material things, getting ahead financially. Matthew 6:33 says, "But seek ye first the kingdom of God, and his righteousness; and all these things shall be added unto you." This they had not been doing.

Making the first step in getting right with God—acknowledging one's failure—they changed the direction of their lives. They began attending the Christian Missionary Alliance Church and made the life altering discovery that God had work for them to do—work that was to shape and guide their lives for the future. Their immediate need, however, was employment for R. G.

A business venture had fared badly, finally necessitating Evelyn's seeking employment. R. G. rebelled. The idea of his wife working was repulsive, but they did pray about it. Shortly thereafter, they learned of a rancher whose ailing wife needed a nursemaid. Evelyn took the job at $40 a month, but there was one hitch. Their respective jobs found them on opposite sides of a canal, close enough to see each other daily, and wave, but the canal was a quarter of a mile wide with the nearest bridge fifteen miles away, and no telephone connections between the two ranches.

R. G. solved the problem on Sundays by rolling up his clothes, tieing them on a raft made of fence posts, and swimming across the canal pushing the raft ahead of him. Again, love found a way!

That was a long summer, and both were happy when a little "sugar shack" became available on the ranch where R. G. was working and Evelyn could once more join him. Never mind the cracks and dust blowing in; they were together and that was all that counted.

R. G.'s mind was forever dreaming up new devices, and he borrowed enough money from his sister Sarah to buy an old tractor. He started leveling land, but didn't like the scrapers. He set about to make his own. That signaled the beginning of the monster earthmoving machines which would bring him world-wide acclaim.

But things were looking better. Financially they felt their heads to be above water, their faith was stronger than ever, and they were together in person and in prayer. It was soon to be Christmas and God was going to bless them with a second child. The hogs were scratching themselves on the iron wheels of the portable cook shack which they called home, and Evelyn was dashing to catch a falling lamp when R. G. walked in the door. "I'm sorry the floor looks so bad," she plaintively said, "I tried to wash the dust off the floor, but I guess I only irrigated it."

On April 2, 1920, their daughter, Louise, was born. R. G.'s days were busy with using his tractor and scraper leveling land. Someone would come along, admire the scraper, and want one. R. G. would sell it, buy some more steel, and build another scraper. This finally resulted in their accumulating enough money to buy an acre of ground. With nothing down and a payment of thirty dollars a month, they had some land and an old house they could call their own. It didn't matter that it lacked running water and plumbing. R. G. was moving more dirt than any one man had ever moved before in history, and more contracts were coming in than he could handle. Besides, they had their health and faith in the Lord.

Their property also boasted an old barn which became headquarters for the business. R. G. used to say, "The barn became my machine shop, the acre of land my open-air factory, and the dust in the driveway my engineering department where, squatting on my heels, I could draw up my 'blueprints' with my finger." The most important part of that venture was declaring God as his partner which gave the two of them great peace of mind.

Evelyn loved being near her husband where she could watch him at work or run errands for him. The latter became a daily necessity. R. G. would order steel in San Francisco one day, have them put it on a boat, and the next morning it would be at the river's edge in Stockton waiting for pickup. Evelyn became his handyman. "Evelyn," he'd come to the kitchen window, knock on it, calling her name. "Forget about the dishes now, drive on over to Higgenbothams, and pick up these things."

She would open the window, and R. G. would thrust in a list of things he needed from the hardware store. With Don, the new baby on her hip, she'd climb into the car, tuck little Louise alongside her, holding onto the baby, and they would prepare to go. R. G. called out at the last moment, "Evelyn, while you're at it, stop at the boat landing and pick up those angle irons too."

Evelyn LeTourneau recalls, "Sometimes I'd have to heat up my dishwater two or three times, but those were happy days because we were working together and I was being a help to him." She was good help—keeping the books, running errands, mothering his children, doing all she could lovingly as his wife.

R. G. was an eighth-grade dropout at fourteen. He had worked as a foundryman, welder, auto mechanic, and electrician while studying automotive mechanics and electrical engineering by correspondence. Evelyn had just enough bookkeeping in high school to be proficient in helping stretch the money. In her attempts to make the money go as far as possible, she had figured out that since it had cost $25 when Louise was born, and it would cost $50 for Don if she had a doctor and went to the hospital, she'd do without the hospital. That way she could have a new dress after the baby's arrival. She was tired of wearing an outsize dress as a maternity dress —washing it out every night in order to have it fresh to wear the next day. Evelyn decided from then on she could help her financial situation by having her babies at home; she didn't need an anesthetic.

Never will she forget the day she asked R. G. if she could drive to town to get some curtain rods for the new curtains she'd just made. R. G. thought seriously for a moment and answered, "Well Evelyn, there's no sense in putting them up on cheap rods; I've got good Tobin bronze rods in the shop. I'll get some for you," and away he went. They worked beautifully.

One day, a few months later, Evelyn came home from town and as she drove in the driveway noticed with dismay that all her curtains were missing. Running into the house, she found them lying in little heaps at the bottom of each window. Hands on her hips she marched out to the barn-workshop, "R. G., where are my Tobin bronze curtain rods?" He looked slightly foolish as he admitted he'd run out of rods and "just happened" to remember that he'd given her some for curtains. They were just what he needed to finish a particular job. Evelyn climbed into the car, drove to town, and bought her own rods. "To this day I've never had Tobin bronze rods," she laughingly declares!

R. G.'s ideas for new machines were constantly getting ahead of his income from land-leveling, welding, and repair work. Busy as those years were, R. G. managed to teach a Sunday school class of teen-age boys. He built a truck and twenty-four-foot trailer which Evelyn could use to cruise around Stockton, collecting kids for Sunday school, or taking them off to Mt. Hermon for summer camp.

Because he was out of town so frequently, they asked Evelyn to take over the class. The following summer she had twenty-six boys going to camp, and a former employee of her husband with a drinking problem. The one-time drunk blurted out one evening following a devotional time, "Evelyn, I need to know how to be saved."

The old streetcar, which R. G. had renovated to haul everyone to camp, became a prayer room next to the shop where employees, Sunday school class boys, and anyone could stop in for counseling and help. Evelyn was always available.

Their son Richard was born in 1925. In 1926 Kaiser Steel came along, having heard of the genius inventor R. G. LeTourneau, and wanted to buy his patent. R. G. acquiesced and agreed to go to work for them. They packed their belongings and moved to Livermore where the Kaiser plant was located.

Now home became a tent. But it was a rather luxurious tent at that with running water, a bathroom, electric stove, washing machine, refrigerator, full-sized bed for the two of them, and two smaller beds for Louise and Donald, and a tiny bed for Richard. It was a temporary living arrangement, but it did make it possible for R. G. to walk to the front gate at Kaiser Steel. But Evelyn was glad when they asked R. G. to move up to Loleta, near Eureka on the coast, to do a job with the scrapers.

While there the LeTourneaus met a gospel team of singing sisters who encouraged them to move to southern California and attend Biola College. For Evelyn it was a rewarding experience which gave valuable insight into how to organize and conduct Sunday schools and summer Bible camps; but for R. G.—a man who had spent his life active in heavy equipment and construction work—it proved too confining. That new venture lasted three months. R. G.'s heart was in his work, and when Kaiser came along and asked him to subcontract another big job, they moved back up to Stockton. This resulted in financial gain so that they could go back into business again. They remodeled their Stockton home, putting in hot and cold running water. Such luxury! And a shop forty by sixty feet became their pride and joy. Now R. G. could really work on his scrapers! Evelyn's heart was singing.

The big event of 1929 was the crash on Wall Street; unnoticed, at the same time, was the founding of R. G. LeTourneau, Inc. On paper they appeared to be worth $127,000. The LeTourneaus got down on their knees and thanked God for his bounty and for sparing them from the business depression that was sweeping the country. That year their son Roy was born. When he was born, the doctor wapped him in a blanket, handed him to his father and said, "R. G., here's your preacher boy." Later, this son was to go to Peru to do pioneer missionary work.

In 1930 they moved to the other side of Stockton and built a large shop. R. G. LeTourneau had established a national reputation as an inventor with over two hundred patents to his credit. He was designing and manufacturing heavy construction equipment—mining, material handling, logging, and land clearing equipment. Another old streetcar was purchased, remodeled into a place the workers could use at lunchtime, and was the first step in the direction of cafeterias for their workers that would one day feed five thousand men.

Their last two children were born in 1932 and 1934. By this time they had outgrown their plants, and it was time to move. In 1935 they moved to Peoria, Illinois. They purchased a piece of land across the river from the Caterpillar dealers, and while Caterpillar made the tractors, the LeTourneau plant manufactured the scrapers. Their move to Peoria was made in a raw spring rain that lasted two weeks without letup. Through all of this Evelyn worked right alongside her husband, a fact which he never forgot.

During the four years they lived in Peoria, Evelyn continued her interest in young people. The homeless crew of fellows who worked for them in California moved right along with them to Illinois. Because she didn't want to turn these fellows loose in a strange city, she rented a big three-story house. Behind the home was an old carriage house with servant quarters. It hadn't been used for a long time, but everyone joined in, fixed it up, moved in beds and furniture, and before she knew what was happening, Evelyn LeTourneau found herself mothering between twenty to thirty boys from all over. The fellows worked for her husband in the plant, but when they came off work they had a warm and cozy place to stay. She hired a cook to feed them. One by one they came to know the Christ she and R. G. loved and served.

These were extremely busy and important days for them. R. G. had little time for anything other than his work, but one day he received a phone call from Arnold Grunigen. "Bob, I want you to come to Chicago and help us kick off a Christian Businessmen's Committee International." R. G. never claimed to be an organizer, but he always stood ready to back and encourage organizations such as this. They made him their chairman. He also became president of Gideons International.

When the LeTourneau Foundation was set up in 1935, they established the fact of giving the dividends on 90 percent of the stock for Christian work and charitable causes. It came about largely because of Evelyn's concern. "Your brother tells me we'll have over a half-million profit this year. Even if we gave half of that away,

106

what can we do with a quarter of a million dollars? The most I've ever spent in my life on the house is $5,000, and well, R. G., it's just too much money."

The foundation was set up to sponsor religious, missionary, and educational work for the greater glory of God; later the LeTourneau's daughter and her husband pioneered missionary work in Africa through foundation grants.

Through the years, as she could, Mrs. LeTourneau accompanied her husband on his many speaking trips both in and out of the country. On one of these trips, May 30, 1937, on their way to Bob Jones College where her husband was to be commencement speaker, they were involved in a serious automobile accident which resulted in five people being killed. R. G. was injured more seriously than his wife; but after that they got an airplane, secured a private pilot, and made trips this way.

August 27, 1937, was their twentieth wedding anniversary. Evelyn persuaded R. G. who was still on crutches from the accident, to accompany her to Winona Lake. She had heard about a camp that was for sale. That was the day she bought Bethany Camp which in the next ten years was to become a home away from home for over two hundred young people from all over the country during the summer months.

Evelyn brought in teachers and counselors from Wheaton College and elsewhere. It was a nondenominational camp with services in the morning, recreation in the afternoon, and services again in the evening. The "Victory Circle" became a place of decision nightly. Evelyn and her children lived at the camp from June to September. Those were happy, memorable years. Today she meets people wherever she goes who say to her, "You may not remember me, but I turned my life over to God at Bethany Camp."

In 1939 they moved to Toccoa, Georgia; and in 1940 their daughter was married. Another home was begun for the boys she managed to "mother," boys who were in a machinist school they had started there.

On the nineteenth of August in 1940 word reached the LeTourneaus that their son Don had crashed in the plane while on a business trip. It was a heartbreaking experience, but once again their faith in God was put to the test and found to be firm.

When they moved to Vicksburg, Mississippi, in 1942, Evelyn plunged into the work of making a home for servicemen. It was wartime.

The move to Longview, Texas, in 1946 resulted in another plant and the founding of LeTourneau College which at the time of this writing has an enrollment of over eight hundred students. It is a Christian coeducational college of engineering, technology, arts and sciences, and flight training. Graduates are being accepted all across the country. One of the finest courses offered is the Missionary Technical Course. Missionaries themselves are trained in Bible schools, but at LeTourneau College they are trained in the art of building houses, fixing cars, repairing airplanes, flying planes, setting up electrical plants, and harnessing water for power use.

Through the years the LeTourneaus so endeared themselves to hundreds of young people that they were called Mom and Pop. Not too long ago Mrs. LeTourneau received a letter from Africa addressed to "Mom," Longview, Texas.

It was a privilege to visit Mrs. R. G. LeTourneau, "Mom," when she was in California late in 1969. Her trip west was prompted by the fact that in May she had been crowned as the American National Mother of the Year, and she was to appear on the Lawrence Welk television program. Just before New Year's Day we again visited. This time she was readying herself to ride in the 1970 Tournament of Roses Parade.

Of her marriage and their life together "Mom" LeTourneau had this to say: "We had a happy marriage of nearly fifty-two years. I have a multitude of wonderful memories. He always said he took a young wife so she could take care of him, but I really enjoyed it. I had great respect and deep love for him.

"After we were married he never bought a suit of clothes, never bought a pair of shoes or anything. I bought all his clothes, and brought them home. If they needed altering, I would take them back to be fixed. When he would get dressed in the morning, I would lay out his clothes for the day, and he never questioned what I did.

"I never asked him to do anything about the house. He was too busy, and I knew I shouldn't be wasting his time. I didn't want him driving across town to the plants either, so we always lived in the part sometimes not considered the nicest part of town, but near to the plant. I didn't even want him driving across or on main highways, because his mind was so busy—he was always thinking of new things to invent.

"It takes real giving for marital happiness. True happiness comes in a oneness with each other and good communication. We started our home with a family altar. This is essential. I shall never forget the time when we were entertaining Chamber of Commerce guests and we had just finished eating. Our youngest boy jumped up and picked up the Bible and brought it to his dad. This was just a family practice—reading the Bible following dinner. My husband read a chapter and we had prayer. Our guests later commented about this—what a beautiful thing and obviously not a 'put on' to impress, but something perfectly natural and a part of our family life.

"We have always gone with our children to Sunday school, not just taken them. Entertaining missionaries, preachers, speakers and having guests in the home—surrounding our children with these influences has been very good. I can't stress enough the importance of summer camp experiences for your children where they learn that their own church isn't the only place where Christian people can be found.

"I am pretty dogmatic about certain things," said the sixty-nine-year-old Texan with quick, well thought-out answers to the multitude of questions I was asking of her. We were moving into discussing how to raise children. The teal gray-haired matron, mother of seven, grandmother of nineteen, and great-grandmother of one, was well qualified to give some good answers.

"Don't criticize each other in front of your children or others. If you have a difference, don't let the children know about it. Talk it out when they are not present.

"Don't criticize the minister either, or the schoolteacher, the Sunday school teacher, or anyone. How can you expect children to show respect if you are critical?

"I have never hesitated to discipline our children. Sparing the rod *is* spoiling the child. When I sold my Bethany Camp, I started a ranch for delinquent boys outside of Longview. I took boys from court or boys considered unmanageable. With few exceptions these boys would tell me their parents didn't care about them—that they never bothered to correct them. They felt because of this lack of discipline that their parents didn't love them. Parents need to exercise correction with love! When you correct a child, go back to that child in a little while, talk it out, and then pray with him. Every child has to be treated as an individual; you can't make ironclad rules that apply to everyone because all of us are different. But a consistency in discipline is essential. This helps to make a child feel secure and loved. And don't threaten to do something and then not carry it out!"

109

Becoming American National Mother of the Year was a real surprise. "A Mrs. Fisher of South Texas, whom I don't even know, called me and asked to submit my name. I gave the okay and then forgot about it. A few weeks later I received word that I had been named Texas Mother of the Year. I came to Los Angeles for the national competition and went on to win."

Each mother had to give a three-minute talk, a synopsis of her life. "I couldn't begin to tell our life story in three minutes," she related, but the deciding factor in her favor came as a result of the way her children have turned out as good Christians following in the lay missionary footsteps of their father, and the fact that she has never received pay for what she has done in her life with the founding and operating of camps and other youth work.

This honor came to her just four weeks before her husband had his fatal stroke. *Christian Times* paper (June 22, 1969) featured an article on R. G. LeTourneau and his death with the headlines "God's Partner Promoted to Home Office."

Yes, God's partner and Evelyn LeTourneau's. Together they had lived a full life in serving God and others. His personal testimony was: "I'm just a mechanic whom the Lord has blessed." Business and his Christian faith were inseparable.

Christian Businessmen's Committee International Executive Secretary, Evon Hedley, at the time of his death, said of him: "He gave not only business, but also all of his spare time to the Lord. He would go anywhere to speak for Jesus Christ. And he would do it at his own expense. One of the outstanding dedicated laymen of our time, he did this when no one else was doing it." And behind him was his wife, a great woman—uncomplaining, cheering him on, matching his zeal with her own, and always loving him for the dear, wonderful husband and father she knew him to be.

At Mr. LeTourneau's funeral, tributes poured in from around the world, and the memorial service held in the Longview gym (the only place large enough to hold the crowd) was a glorious occasion. Today the plant and college at Longview carry on. The oldest son, Richard, is president of the company. At his father's funeral Richard spoke of their great gratitude for the past and their father's example, but now they were to look to the future and carry on as he would have wanted them to do. Roy is head of the Sales Department; Ted takes after his famous father in designing and engineering as head of the Engineering Department; and the youngest son, Ben, on leave of absence, graduated from Texas A&M in May, 1970.

"Mom" LeTourneau continues to represent the Lord and carry on the "partnership with God" faith of her husband to which she so wholeheartedly subscribes. As Mother of the Year she is frequently asked: What shall we do about our young people and the breakdown of the family structure?

Her answers: "Start disciplining children the day they are born; don't wait until they give you trouble.

"Educate women to be mothers, not everything else.

"Never go to bed angry.

"Read the Bible and pray together at night on your knees.

"You can't make your husband over, you can't make him good, but you can make him happy." This from the one-time pig-tailed little girl who had run to her room crying, "Oh God, let Bob LeTourneau wait for me."

# Barbara Hancock Fain

### wife of COLONEL JOHN FAIN

The convertible pulled up in front of the Brookhaven Country Club, but the beautiful woman behind the steering wheel didn't budge. Others going into or leaving the club couldn't possibly know that Barbara Fain was having a time of real introspection. The struggle had begun some time before, but reached a climax of soul-searching as she sat—motionless—in her car, facing facts head on.

What were those facts? What thoughts were crashing in upon her, colliding and jarring into her sensitive conscience a realization that would change her destiny?

Barbara Fain was knowledgeable of parts of the Bible. She had seen in her husband a change so dramatic that she had thought: Isn't it wonderful when someone wants to be so "religious." But still she questioned his changed life and wondered: He seems to have gotten old all of a sudden . . . he's no more fun. And then she'd catch herself thinking: Or is it age? He's reading the Bible. It sent her into the Bible to try to see for herself what he was finding.

That day, climbing the Atlanta social ladder, and going to the club seemed quite unimportant, as she reflected: I call myself a Christian. I believe in Jesus Christ—or do I? Yes, I do, intellectually at least. Sure, I believe in the fact of Jesus' historicity.

Disturbing thoughts. More than a little unsettling. After all, she thought, I've mentally planned our little daughter's social debut; I've programmed my life pretty successfully. But the arguments choked in her throat as she tried verbalizing her feelings to herself.

And now, here she was. Why didn't she get out of the car, go into the club, and have a good time with her friends? Questions. What's the matter with you, Barbara? Facts. You know you can't control your own life and at the same time have Christ in the center of your life. Either Jesus Christ is going to be Lord and Savior, or you're going to be your own Lord and Savior.

The investigation of the inner woman continued: Now what good is it going to do me to live my life and when I die I'll be separated from God? I know enough about the Bible to know that separation from God will be a terrible thing. Hmmmm . . .

Barbara Fain didn't like anybody clouding issues for her regardless what the issue was. She wasn't easy on herself and allowed the interrogation to proceed: You know all about hell, Barbara, and there's only one destiny for you as things stand right this moment. This is ridiculous. But the Bible says what will it profit a man if he gain the whole world and lose his own soul.

"God, I give myself and my life to your Son, Jesus Christ."

The struggle was over. Barbara looked around her and out the car window. Was the sun shining earlier? Was the day so beautiful before? Peace. The inner clamor was gone. She was now a Christian.

In the days that followed, as she read the Bible, she vacillated between, "Well, I wonder if I am or if I'm not a Christian." And then, God brought to her attention Romans 10: "That if thou shalt confess with thy mouth the Lord Jesus, and shalt believe in thine heart that God hath raised him from the dead, thou shalt be saved."

Eagerly she read the entire chapter. "For with the heart man believeth unto righteousness; and with the mouth confession is made unto salvation. For the Scripture saith, Whosoever believeth on him shall not be ashamed." That week Barbara's social calendar called for her to attend a beautiful brunch on the north side of Atlanta. She made up her mind that she'd talk to everybody about the Lord. She determined to put into practice exactly what those Bible verses said a believer was to do.

Barbara Fain explains her first faltering attempts like this: "I'm sure I said all the wrong things, but the Lord is so gracious. He looks right to the heart." And, true to her nature, she shared joyously what God was revealing to her from his Word.

This Christian experience was precipitated by the following heartcry one night, after reading the Bible, when she had gotten on her knees and confessed: "God, I don't believe I love you with all my heart the way you tell me to because I love my husband more than I love you. I can see him, and I can't see you; but, God, if you will show me how to love you the most, I will."

What happened in answer to that prayer was revolutionary to her thinking. Barbara, like many individuals, considered herself good by the world's standards. "I compared myself with man's standards of goodness. But God showed me his standard was his Son. When I compared myself with Jesus Christ, I fell far short. With this comparison, directed by the Holy Spirit, I realized what it really means to be a sinner."

Her desire to share Christ and the Bible led her quite naturally to her family and old friends. The reaction among some was, "Why Barbara, you've always been a good Christian girl." What was her past like?

Barbara Hancock was the youngest in a family of seven. Her father was a country doctor before Oklahoma gained statehood. Then he went into the ginning business and patented the first ribless cotton gin. She was born in Wapanucka, Oklahoma, in 1924. Most of her growing-up years were spent in Oklahoma City. Her father was a good man, quiet and gentle; her mother was a very courageous woman who stamped upon her daughter's life a richness of character that is immediately evident. Her home was a Christian home, and by the time Barbara was eight years old, she had read the Bible through and attended daily vacation Bible schools and Sunday school.

Barbara's seeking personality led her to investigate every church in Oklahoma City on her own at the age of fifteen. Once when she was asked if she believed on the Lord Jesus Christ she replied, "Well, of course. Doesn't everybody?" She even insisted on being baptized twice!

While attending the University of Oklahoma, she majored in drama, which interest was the major thrust of her life at that time. She also worked as a model. When bombs were dropped on Pearl Harbor December 7, 1941, Barbara's education, like that of many others, was interrupted. The popular thing, of course, was to help in the war effort.

She became the private classified secretary for the chief of training for the Oklahoma City Air Service Command. In her heart, however, she nurtured the dream and had made some tentative plans to go to California where her sister lived and pursue her drama career. Studies at the Pasadena Playhouse sounded mighty exciting; but meanwhile, Barbara and the girls in the office were having the time of their lives dating the young men that came through.

Barbara had decided, however, that she wasn't going to get involved with anyone who was going to be sent overseas to war. She had friends whose husbands had already been killed. No thanks, she thought, this isn't for me. But she was having fun! "All the girls would get together when a new group of fellows came through. We'd each pick out the one we wanted to date. On March 14, 1944, this group of staff officers from the Pentagon came through. I saw this tall, dashing officer with beautiful black hair and a dark little moustache and singled him out; but he didn't know it!"

Barbara's husband tells it like this: "When I walked into the office, I noticed this little blonde head with hair hanging down on her shoulders—kind of bobbing up and down, you know, while she was going to work on that typewriter. I was kind of a smart-aleck, so I went up behind her and got a little of the hair in my hand, rubbed it through my fingers, and thought I would tease her.

"She didn't stop typing—but she knew I was standing back of her and she knew what I was doing, but she acted real coy. So I asked her, 'Listen, sweetheart, I want to know the truth. Is this real or have you been putting peroxide on it?' When I said that, she turned around and looked me straight in the eye and flashed her blue eyes into my eyes and boy, my heart flipped! Been flipping ever since! So, we made a date. And I asked her to make dates for all my staff.

"We went out that night and had a delightful time. On the way

115

home in the taxi I knew I was going to marry her. . . ." Forty days later they were married!

Barbara Fain explains: "We were meant for each other and have always been deeply grateful to the Lord for working it out, even though it was an unusually short courtship. God saw that we should be together even before we were Christians."

It was a beautiful May day in 1944 when they said their "I do's" in a lovely chapel decorated with big urns of varicolored tulips. After the wedding the groom whisked his beautiful bride away on the train to Washington, D.C., where he had an apartment.

Barbara recalls that she learned everything after marriage out of books. "I learned how to cook from books; later, after we'd moved to Tampa, Florida, where my husband was stationed at Drew Field, and our daughter, Jackie, was born I purchased a baby book and followed the instructions to the letter!

"In the same way I learned to know the voice of God after coming to Christ, and to hear him talk to me through the Bible. As a youngster I loved to read, not only to read the words, but I learned to assimilate the knowledge that was there."

This love of reading became the influential force in her life, leading her to seek out for herself the truths from the Bible which led to her becoming a Christian without outside help. It also led to her becoming one of the most sought-after Bible teachers in the South and on the East Coast in the years that were to follow.

In September, 1946, after having served on General "Hap" Arnold's staff in Washington for two years, Colonel Fain entered General Hospital for treatment of nervous fatigue and facial paralysis. Actually his troubles were the result of a spinal injury sustained in a plane accident in 1944 in which he could have lost his life.

The Fains moved to Atlanta, Georgia. He was now retired from active military service, and they purchased a home. As the son of a well-known Atlanta family, the Colonel felt he was really returning home. His military career had spanned many years of active service in which he had distinguished himself in the Pacific Theater of Operations as a member of General Douglas MacArthur's Fifth Air Force Staff. When he retired, it was with the rank of Colonel.

His physical problem, however, still troubled him, and so he submitted to treatment at the Oliver General Hospital in Augusta. With his wife and daughter settled in their new home, he left for what he thought would be a brief hospital stay. Enroute, the Colonel had a most unusual experience. "As I turned a curve, I happened to look up. Right there some crackpot had nailed a sign on a tree. It said: Repent, for the kingdom of heaven is at hand. I cursed the man who put that up because I thought it was religious bunk. But the Spirit of God did his work in my life. As I read the sign, it was as if God had pulled a spiritual veil from my mind and heart. I knew he was talking to me. I became convicted that I was alienated from God.

"I went on down the highway a little further and turned another curve. That same religious crackpot had put up another sign. It said: Today is the day of salvation; now is the accepted time. For the first time I saw an urgency in my being rightly related to God.

"I drove on into the grounds of the hospital and found that this same crackpot had put another sign up, and it had just two words on it: Eternity where? I had to answer that question right there—eternity for me, in my lost condition, was to be forever away from God. I was deeply concerned and convicted that I was lost.

"I went into the hospital thinking all I'd do was sign my name and wait two or three days for retirement orders and then go home. But they had different plans for me. The doctors decided to tap my spine and put me in traction again. There I was, back in bed again with weights on my head, and my feet hoisted up in the air. All I could do was lie there and look up. While I was lying there, it was as if I was looking into a mirror—God's mirror. I saw my reflection as he saw me, a lost condemned sinner without any purpose in life, without any hope. As I lay there, I knew I must do something about it.

"After two weeks I was released from the hospital and started back to Atlanta. That same crackpot had put some signs on the other side of the road. I became so under conviction of sin that I actually felt sick. There is no sickness like sin-sickness and there's only one cure for it, and that's Jesus Christ."

Colonel John Fain invited Jesus Christ to take over his life and he's never been the same. John Fain had been known as the international playboy—an extremely handsome, carefree, happy, intelligent, and wealthy man who could rent a yacht and take off with friends for a Caribbean holiday. His change was dramatic indeed!

His love and dedication as a Christian were exemplary. When he made a commitment, it was a commitment all the way. Nothing was held back and God began to bless him uniquely and use him in a wonderful way.

117

Barbara was taking notice of her husband's change—he no longer drank, he stopped smoking, his language cleaned up, and he dropped speaking profanities. Her friends were teasing her about being married to an old Colonel (he was fifteen years her senior). But she was searching the Bible herself trying to determine what it was that had made the difference in her husband. She read: "If any man be in Christ, he is a new creature." That description fit her husband!

And that resulted in Barbara's encounter with Christ in front of the country club. She saw that her parental religious heritage was no substitute for a personal relationship with Jesus Christ. She had been "religious" and God-conscious, but now she became Christ-conscious.

The Fains began attending a Bible-believing church where the pastor, Reverend T. J. Spier, told them to get a good chain-reference Bible, a topical textbook, and a concordance and get busy studying the Word. Some days Barbara would study twelve hours straight. She explains, "I had an insatiable hunger to know Christ better."

As they worked prayerfully together to establish a Christian home, God was working to open other doors of witness and service. John Fain was now in the insurance and real estate business; but in his three-story office building he sold Christian assurance, too, and his clients not only bought homes on earth, but they heard about a heavenly home that could be theirs by faith alone.

In Atlanta, as elsewhere in the country, every real estate company prospered after the war, but few grew like the Colonel's. In a business where Sunday selling was the popular thing to do, John Fain refused to do business on the Lord's Day.

Half of his office building became a permanent house of God—most of the second-floor was a prayer room. Offices for the Atlanta Youth for Christ were quartered on the third floor. Atop the building was a three-sided, sixty-foot sign. Each side sent out the same bright red message in neon, "Jesus Saves." The sign was so large it could be read from half of the hotel rooms in the city, from the Y.M.C.A., and dozens of downtown office buildings, and three main state highways. If highway signs could be effective in drawing him to seek the Lord, the Colonel was determined that others be given the same opportunity. Barbara Fain will never forget the day the sign was first lit up. "The street was closed off and there were hundreds of people who had gathered. When they pulled the switch and the sign came on for the very first time, everyone joined in singing *All Hail the Power of Jesus' Name,* and it was a very precious time. The presence of the Lord was very, very real."

Colonel Fain became a very active layman, much in demand across the country for speaking engagements. Early in his experience with Christ he came home one day from his office and said, "Honey, God just showed me something. I just witness all the time and tell people about Christ but nobody's ever saved. I believe you have to get them on the dotted line just like you do when you sell a piece of property. The next time I'm going to do more than tell them about Christ; I'm going to ask them to invite Christ in, to receive him, to accept him as their personal Savior."

So he did. He began to lead people to the Lord right and left—everywhere. Barbara explains, "I figured as I watched my husband, well, if he can do that, I know God can use me, too. So emulating his example, I began to see that you can share your faith with others. And the Lord really blessed. God just overlooked the non-professional, uncool way that we did this. Our efforts were so sincere—right from our hearts."

So outstanding was Barbara's way with people that John Fain volunteered her services to the then Atlanta Bible Institute (which is now a Christian academy) where she taught a course on personal evangelism. Barbara was deeply humbled and prayed, "God, you are the real soul winner, but I'm willing to be your servant. You're just going to have to show me how to make this effective." He did!

Barbara Fain feels, however, that the greatest thing God did for her after she became a spirit-filled Christian was to give her a heart's desire to make their home truly Christ centered. "We grew up in a generation where there was not communication of one's faith—you went to church, you read the Bible, and you prayed, but you didn't talk much about how Christ could meet one's every need. As a result, many children could quote Scripture and tell Bible stories, but they were just little rascals and didn't know how to live and apply the Christian life. I didn't want our daughter to turn out like that.

"I wanted Jackie, our daughter, to be God's woman. I wanted God's wisdom to teach her. Day by day, as I read the Bible I'd think: This is so great because I can use this Bible story to teach Jackie this particular truth. The mother is such a responsible person in the area of raising small children."

Two things Barbara and John Fain did after they became Chris-

119

tians—they read the Bible together every morning and had prayer, then in the evening they read a Bible story to their daughter. From the time they became vital Christians, they prayed that Jackie would come to know Christ at an early age. In her presence they would pray: Lord, we just pray that Jackie will come to know and love you.

When their daughter was four years old she did respond to discipline meted out rather severely by her mother as punishment for picking flowers without permission. She learned in a very real way what it meant to be a sinner, alienated from her parents as a result of wrongdoing. Barbara Fain, wise mother that she was, used the episode to relate to the child what it means to be separated from God, our Heavenly Father, because of hearts that are "black with sin."

When little Jackie prayed, in her parents' presence, asking God to wash away her sin and inviting Jesus into her heart's house, she knew exactly what she was doing. After that she went around to everyone she met telling them, "I've asked Jesus into my heart." Barbara looked at this only child God had blessed her with and remembered the story of the virtuous woman in Proverbs 31. "I realized that a Christian woman is great if her husband is known and her children call her blessed. That's what I wanted—that was the real desire of my heart. If I had a goal it would be that my husband be known in the gate (as the Bible expresses it) as a man of God, and that my daughter would love Christ."

It was wonderful to the Fain family to realize that God was moving in all their lives at the same time. Opportunities for service as a family were coming in from all over. John Fain was widely sought after as a speaker. Because he had been with General Douglas MacArthur, had been a staff officer and a psychological warfare officer and because he had an unusual and aggressive Christian testimony, he was much in demand.

But wherever he went, the colonel took along his family. He would say to those who invited him to their city, "You know, my wife teaches Bible classes. So please arrange for her to have Bible classes each morning while we are there." And then Jackie would play the piano. She began to take lessons when she was five and would play "Sun of My Soul" or some little hymn. Barbara says, "That would be her part. She always shared in the ministry. She was never separated from what we were doing. We would pray together about these various services, and so her part was to be obedient and pray. We taught her that's what her ministry as a child was."

Barbara also taught her a simple plan of salvation called the ABC's of the Gospel: admit that you're a sinner; believe that Jesus died for you; and confess him as your Lord. They taught her the Bible verses to go with that and gave her a little Testament. She grew up knowing how to lead others to Christ.

When as a child their daughter was asked what she wanted for Christmas, she would reply, "I want to go to a Billy Graham Crusade." For birthday parties she would ask her mother to tell her friends Child Evangelism stories, and many decisions were made for Christ as a result. When she became a teen-ager, she would have slumber parties and read the Bible and pray with her friends. In high school she was active in the Student Christian Fellowship.

Many honors were heaped upon Jackie Fain—she was consistently described as "a popular student with numerous campus organization memberships and leadership positions." She was a cheerleader, senior superlative, "Miss Teen-age Atlanta," and finalist in the 1963 "Miss Teen-age America" pageant, homecoming queen, a talented pianist and soloist with the Atlanta Pops Concert Orchestra—but through it all she maintained a consistent Christian witness. She attended Wheaton College and Florida State where she was instrumental in getting a Campus Crusade for Christ group organized.

It was because of Jackie's interest in Campus Crusade that Dr. Bill Bright, its founder, came to Atlanta to conduct a Lay Institute in May 1965. There Dr. Bright met the Fain family who faithfully attended the lectures and seminars. After one such meeting John Fain said to his wife, "You know, this would really work in the military."

Later, when they mentioned this to Dr. Bright, he replied, "I've been praying that God would give us a man to begin this work in the military service." They all began to pray about it. And then God began to perform a succession of what appeared to the Fains to be miracles! First of all, God gave them real direction from the Scriptures that this is what he wanted them to do; and then, he directed in the selling of property which would enable them to go into the military work.

Colonel Fain became National Director of the Military Ministry of Campus Crusade for Christ, International, in January of

1966. Barbara's role has been to assist him by training the military staff women, speaking at retreats and meetings when invited, and traveling extensively with her husband, working also with military staff women on installations where they have been assigned. This has been a pioneer work for Campus Crusade that has seen the Fains working and praying to employ strategy that enables them to most ably assist military chaplains at their invitation. God has blessed.

Their daughter, now married to businessman Jerry Curtis Nims, travels around the world with her husband as associate staff members for Campus Crusade presenting a musical-prose program entitled "Fantasia in Red, White, and Blue." Jackie originated the program which is designed to honor the servicemen and women of America and is dedicated to the wives and mothers of fighting men overseas. Its purpose is to focus attention of citizens on allegiance to our country, to introduce men and women to the historical person Jesus Christ and to tell them how one may know him personally, to assist military chaplains, and to challenge commitment to Christian principles.

Barbara Fain says, "When I came to Christ, he gave me a love and appreciation for other people I'd never had before because I was so independent, self-centered and self-sufficient. But God took this and tempered it by the Holy Spirit's control and gave me an interest in and concern for other people. He truly freed me from the small island of myself.

"My husband has so many wonderful and unique qualities—but supremely what stands out is his love for people. He just loses his identity in helping others. He is an intensely loyal man. As I watched him, I learned from him. Then, as I read the Bible, I knew God wanted me to teach Bible studies. My husband had to put up with a lot from me because I was so strong willed. But I learned when he made decisions that they were really directed by God, and that my husband was my head—just as the Bible says one's husband is to be. He has had a unique ministry, especially in the last three decades, and is a man that has been greatly used of God. Our lives have been rich and full as together we've lived before the Lord, endeavoring to know God's perfect will."

Colonel Fain, with the love of which his wife speaks showing so radiantly, comments: "I've had lots of thrills in my life. I had everything that money could buy. I had social position, military rank, and some honors from the military establishment. But the greatest thrill to me is when I see an honest seeking man or woman who does not know the Lord Jesus Christ come to him in faith, and when the light of the gospel becomes real to the man and breaks over his countenance—that's the greatest thrill one can possibly experience.

"I told somebody recently, 'My friend Billy Graham has his team, but I've had my home-grown team.' God has given us a wonderful ministry as a family together.

"My wife is one of the finest Bible teachers in the country, and although I didn't go to seminary, I've had the seminary in my home as God has used Barbara to teach me his word."

# Hannah Thompson

## mother of ROBERT N. THOMPSON

The table was beautifully set. The snow-white linen tablecloth had been painstakingly ironed and the best china carefully arranged at each place. Fresh coffee was brewing, the aroma tempting everyone who entered the door—you knew it was freshly ground coffee. Food steamed from the big bowls placed down the center of the table. Bustling around and hovering anxiously over all the beforehand preparations and the serving was a pert, barely five-foot tall, dark-haired, beautiful young woman. Her eyes flashed the satisfaction she could not conceal. She loved entertaining. Even the threshing crew!

Was ever a group of hard working farmers entertained so well?

The threshing crew enjoyed coming to the Thompson farm—Hannah's reputation in the kitchen was well known. It may have been in the days before the maxim "the hostess with the mostest" became famous, but it could have been aptly applied to the young Mrs. Thompson. Nowhere in all the district were the threshers served off a white linen tablecloth!

Mrs. Ted Thompson's baking and cooking skills were unexcelled, whether it was her Swan's Down angel food cakes, sponge cakes, freshly baked brownbread, molasses gingersnaps, or meatballs. She rightly fulfilled the biblical exhortation "given to hospitality."

The provinces of British Columbia and Alberta in Canada invite the use of superlatives—from the mountain forests down to the foothill ranges with their grazing cattle and corrals of rodeo and thoroughbred horses; with uncluttered horizons, sunsets that defy description, and anonymous miles of prairies. But to the eyes of young Hannah Thompson the beauties of Canada went virtually unnoticed. She was homesick. Lonesome. Her aching longing for her native Wisconsin was real. Wasn't Wisconsin beautiful too with its dells, rivers, rushing waterfalls, wooded trails, and scenic beauty? Or Minnesota. How she missed Duluth! Yes, the cities—that was it; she missed the cities.

It was true. Hannah Thompson was a city girl. Pioneer life in the Canadian wilderness early in 1918 was a far cry from that to which she had been accustomed in Eau Claire, Wisconsin, where she had been born and raised.

One of Hannah's first jobs as a young girl took her into the employ of a millionaire lumberman and his wife until she decided to go to business college.

At the end of her training at Eau Claire Business College, she sallied forth into the harsh business world. In Duluth she found employment with the Underwood Typewriter people. Pictures of that era show a slightly built girl posing alongside a sleighful of Underwood typewriters. She was Miss Underwood of 1911! The picture was widely circulated in advertising promotion. No wonder! Miss Olufson enhanced the appeal of the Underwood typewriter!

She lived with her sister and husband. One day her sister said, "Hannah, I've got a boyfriend for you."

Saucily tipping her head, Hannah replied, "I'll pick my own, thank you!"

Soon thereafter her sister asked her to go to the corner store.

Unknown to Hannah, they had invited the eligible and strikingly good-looking Ted Thompson to dinner, and he conveniently arrived while Hannah was off to the store.

In his words, "Hannah came hippity-hoppety home, bouncing into the living room. There I was, sitting on the couch." She was startled into momentary speechlessness. The young man sitting on the couch had dark hair and was as dapper and dashing a fellow as she had ever seen. Young Thompson found the words sticking in his throat also . . . if she wasn't the brightest, prettiest little thing, well—

Running into the kitchen Hannah blurted out, "Dora, you mean thing!" Mean or not, it was the beginning of a relationship that, at the time of this writing, had already endured fifty-seven years as man and wife.

It was a happy courtship of ice-skating and skiing dates in the winter months and swimming in the summer. Hannah's eyes still shine as she remembers the figure eights and backward skating on the Duluth frozen lakes, and the eight o'clock in the morning and four o'clock in the afternoon swimming dates!

When things got serious, Hannah's sister decided to teach this happy-go-lucky little wisp of a sister how to cook. Quickly, Hannah learned the art of making angel food cakes. If the way to a man's heart was really through his stomach, she was going to learn all she could! She was a determined little go-getter! On August 11, 1913, they were married.

Ted Thompson's civil service employment seemed as secure and stable a job as a woman could desire for the man she was to marry. But there was a restlessness about young Ted, a yearning for something different. "Hannah, let's visit Canada."

He couldn't forget Canada. His parents were among the early settlers in Western Canada. Rugged pioneers they were, braving the wilds with strong wills, settling near Markerville, not too far from the Medicine and Red Deer Rivers. The towering woodlands nearby, with their majestic trees falling silently into the bottomless moss and fern-shadowed canyons, had left an indelible mark upon young Ted's thinking. The endless prairies were calling forth the more hearty who would homestead, break the sod, and transform the countryside. Ted knew it would call for stamina, but he was confident he possessed it, and his fiery little Hannah seemed equal.

They visited his parents. Upon returning, Hannah said, "I didn't mind visiting, but I'd sure hate to live there." Then she described

126

the muddy roads, the travel sixteen miles from town by horse and buggy that seemed like a hundred miles! To her mother she confided, "I don't want to live on a farm. I don't want to go to Canada."

Hannah's mother looked at her daughter and said, "You go where your husband wants to go."

And so they went. A boxcar was loaded with their furniture and belongings, and the Thompsons boarded the train. With them was their two-year-old son, Robert, and baby daughter, Grace. At International Falls they encountered difficulties with identification papers. Silently Hannah hoped they'd get sent back to Duluth. Finally they were allowed to go on after a prolonged uncomfortable overnight wait.

It was a year before Hannah Thompson was to see the lights of a city again, and when she did she was heard to say, "Ohhh, I hear a train whistle . . . ohhh, I see the lights of a town!"

The years ahead after settling near Innisfail in southwestern Canada were to prove long and difficult. The first year it was said of Hannah Thompson that she put ten years on her pretty face. At first Ted and Hannah lived with his parents until a neighborhood "building bee" got together, and within a week the men in the district had built for them a home across the section just before their second son, Howard, was born.

Isolated in the Canadian wilderness and feeling very lonely, Hannah Thompson was really not alone. She had been born into a Christian home June 3, 1892, and the Christian influence had left its mark. By the time she was a girl of fifteen, she had recognized the claim that Christ had upon her life. Now, far from loved ones and all that was familiar, she found herself drawn closer to this One whose promises she knew from reading the Bible. Over and over to herself she repeated, "Not alone, not alone—He's ever near, He's ever near." With this she was comforted.

When death came into the home taking their daughter Grace, Hannah wept but did not give up. Little Grace was with Jesus, and Hannah was expecting their fourth child. A few days after burying Gracie, son Grant was born.

Two years after the birth of son Grant, another daughter was born. Hannah was happy. Little Arlone was a sweet child. The last child to bless the family home was another son, George.

Sundays were special. On Thursday Hannah began her Sunday preparations. This meant baking her famous cakes. On Saturday afternoons she would send one of the children to a neighbor's home to invite them over for Sunday afternoon. Out would come the two and a half-gallon ice cream freezer, and everyone took turns turning the crank. Nothing tasted better than homemade ice cream and Hannah's cake. By Monday there wasn't even a cake crumb left.

In the summer of 1927 when the Thompsons acquired their first Model "T" car, Hannah decided that she was going to go for a drive. The men were harvesting and threshing on a neighbor's farm. She had never been behind the steering wheel before, but she had watched her good friend Mrs. Hummer drive her husband's earlier model. Together the two of them kept busy with Bethel Ladies' Aid, and Hannah had ridden alongside her neighbor several times. Her friend wore a helmet with goggles and big gloves on her hands. Hannah possessed none of these but was undaunted.

"Howard," she said to her young son, "you take the car out of the garage and we'll go to town." Howard's mouth opened wide in amazement. He was eight years old!

Somehow this little fellow managed to get the car out of the garage without mishap. "Now Howard, you sit on the floor and feed it the gas, and I'll steer it." Off they went! Unfortunately, a lady living on the road along which they were traveling was dubbed Mrs. Gab-a-lot by the family for her obvious bad habit! As they drove along Hannah observed, "Oh dear, I see Mrs. Gab-a-lot is on the porch."

"Mom," answered little Howard sitting on the car floorboard, "just keep your eyes on the road, please!"

A little further on Hannah said, "Howard, do you suppose any-one else is looking?" It was all Howard could do to keep feeding the gas, and anyway, how was he supposed to know, sitting on the floor—mothers can be so dumb, he thought silently!

But someone else was looking! It was her husband and son Bob! Out in the field, loading the bundle rack, Bob called out, "Hey Dad, would you look at that . . . someone's driving the car." They both paused, wiped the perspiration from their faces, and then Bob screamed out, "Oh no! It's Mother." There was nothing the two of them could do. Later Hannah was to explain, "I got tired of being home."

Another neighbor, driving his team of horses along the narrow road, saw the approaching vehicle. Recognizing the car, he peered closely to see who was behind the wheel; and when he saw it was tiny Hannah Thompson, he drove his horses right into the ditch. He wasn't taking any chances! It was a hair-raising experience Howard was never to forget. It was the one and only time Hannah ever drove a car.

The Thompsons lived on the farm ten years before Hannah reconciled herself to the fact that they were there to stay. Then, and then only, did she want her husband to plant any trees or shrubberies on the place. As I walked about the farm in midwinter 1970 with the now elderly Thompsons at my side, I couldn't help admiring the magnificent stand of stately Russian poplars, spruces, evergreens, elms, and maples that surrounded the property—all planted by Mr. Thompson and his sons.

Mrs. Thompson pointed to a wide expanse, "That was the ball diamond where all the community young people would play and eat ice cream and cake afterwards." It was not difficult to visualize the excitement and fun of such occasions.

We walked to the original old farmhouse, vacated by the family twenty-seven years ago when they moved into a new home on the property some hundred yards to the north. Memories were crowding in. . . .

Earlier I had seen other survivors of the past, as we had driven through the countryside—tall grain elevators like lighthouses alongside rail-lines, towns cluttered by decay, old buildings and homes casting shadows against each other, places that held memories for the driver of our car.

Robert N. Thompson, member of the Canadian Parliament, had met our plane at Calgary. My teen-age daughter accompanied me; we were delighted at the prospect of meeting such a distinguished gentleman, and we were thrilled at the idea of going on up into Canada and seeing a farm. We, too, were city gals!

But who was this Robert N. Thompson, and who was the little woman behind him? As we drove through the Canadian countryside I was to learn much. My reading had already supplied me with sufficient information to know that he was a dynamic statesman and a dedicated godly man.

As Conservative Member of Parliament for his home constituency of Red Deer, Alberta, Canada, his perspective of international problems had been unusually broadened by fifteen years he spent in Ethiopia as special advisor to Emperor Haile Selassie. This had been furthered by wide travels through Europe, Latin America, India, the Far East, Australia, and New Zealand. He was a recognized authority in the fields of education, international relations, and particularly on the people and history of Africa. As a prolific speaker he averages more than two hundred public speaking engagements yearly across Canada and the United States, addressing university audiences, civic and service clubs, church organizations, and political gatherings. The day before meeting us he had been at the Presidential Prayer Breakfast in Washington, D.C., and had conferred with the president and others on the situation in Biafra.

Only days before that he had returned from a six-day, fact-finding tour to the troubled country of Nigeria, much of that time spent in what had been rebel territory.

His articles and writings have appeared frequently in religious, educational, and geographic journals. Where does a man learn courage and honesty and develop the working drive that enables him to carry on such a vigorous life?

My questions were to find answers as I listened and learned while spending time with the Thompsons and their illustrious sons.

In 1919 young Bob started to school in the typical one-room country schoolhouse known to so many Canadians. In later years he was to return to the very same school and become its teacher with forty-three pupils and nine grades! Two of his pupils were to be his brothers Howard and Grant whom he made call him, as teacher, Mr. Thompson. Of that experience his brother Howard states, "That was the trial of Bob's life!"

As a prolific reader Bob soon knew Canadian, American, and British history. Gladstone, Wilberforce, Lincoln, and others had special interest for him. He learned his school lessons well, but also learned the value of hard work—rising early to help with farm chores, and then going on to school.

The consistency of his mother's devotional life did not escape his inquiring gaze. Nightly prayers at his bedside were regular.

When Bob's sister Grace died, his mother took him aside and explained that Gracie was safe in the arms of Jesus, and because this was true she had that song sung at the memorial service. He never forgot it and took courage from watching his mother handle her grief.

Still later, when the second and last little daughter Arlone died, Hannah Thompson was grief-stricken at the loss. Yet she maintained her belief that God was in control and told her children there was a reason for everything. As she talked she explained that the tragedies of life were hard, but God could use such experiences to mold his people. She would go outside, walk around the farm, and repeat, "Hannah, you're not alone—God's ever near." Indeed, in later years when deep personal tragedy was to strike Robert Thompson and his wife, he was to remember those childhood experiences of early grief.

The Thompson home in the original country place is a haven for this busy eldest son who never fails to stop, trying to get there every two weeks as he commutes by plane from his own home in Ottawa. Today he is considered the top expert on African and Southeast Asian affairs in the Canadian parliament.

When everyone gathers at the old Thompson farmstead with Hannah and Ted, there are seventeen grandchildren and two great grandchildren in addition to the sons and their wives. The family remains close to one another, a dedicated Christian group.

The walls of the old home are well lined with pictures—Bob with His Excellency, the Right Honourable George P. Vanier, D.S.O., M.C., C.D., late Governor General of Canada; Bob with General Ky, Vice President and Prime Minister of South Vietnam; Bob with Emperor Haile Selassie of Ethiopia; Bob with Biafran refugees; Howard in his scarlet tunic of the RCMP; Grant, a graduating doctor; and other family photos.

There are wall mottoes too which reflect the manner of living of the occupants of the home: Jesus Never Fails; In All Thy Ways Acknowledge Him, Proverbs 3:6; and others. There are many old religious paintings, scrapbooks filled with other pictures. and voluminous newspaper and magazine clippings. And nowadays the television brings their son right into the living room, as does the radio with regularity.

Ted Thompson has always said his wife spends more money on postage than any woman in the country; but from the mail I saw spilling over on the buffet, and the cards standing around, it was obvious Hannah Thompson has many friends around the world who remember her often!

Hannah Thompson keeps up with everything political with a mind as sharp and alert as the days of her spirited youth.

Several years ago she had tea with President Nixon's mother, then living in Whittier, California. It was one of the real highlights of her life. Their travels have taken them to distant places, and they know Ottawa and Washington intimately.

As her elder son has become well known nationally and internationally, Hannah has increased her praying, though she has always led a consistent prayer life. "Knowing the strenuous work he has, the great responsibilities thrust upon him, I feel the greater necessity to hold him up. It is an empty life for those who don't know how to pray, I am sure," she states with implicit confidence born from long years of praying and seeing answered prayer.

The most important contribution a mother can make in the lives of her children, she feels, "is to bring them up as Christians." This she has done well with her own sons.

"Mothers today must set examples for their children that are worthy of being followed," she maintains. "Yet so many of their lives are anything but that which their children should be seeing. How can they expect their children to turn out good?" she asks.

"Give them responsibility when they are young. I always saw to it that they had regular chores both before and after school. I didn't keep the woodbox full—they did!"

She still bakes her brown bread, molasses cookies, animal cookies with pink icing, and angel foods! She still takes great pleasure in entertaining, though not as often anymore. Her husband is retiring more and more into his old rocker across from hers. But little Hannah darts around with great spirit and lots of vim. In years past every visitor who came to the home left with some baked goods in a brown paper bag, or a jar of her famous preserves. In more recent years she thrusts into the hands of departing visitors a lovely piece of English bone china. Thus it was, as we left, we carried a tangible evidence of Hannah Thompson's love and thoughtfulness, not with one piece of china, but a lovely tea set and several other pieces. She loves to give, but in so doing she gives mainly of herself. For who could forget her love and beautiful spirit!

Our visit together was drawing to a close. It had been special. As we sat in her cheery kitchen suddenly Hannah Thompson's delicate little hand flew to her mouth and she startled us with an, "Oh!" Her son Grant said, "Now what?"

"Do you know," she said, "I forgot to use my white linen tablecloth for our guest!" No one had noticed but the little city-girl-turned Canadian wilderness wife and mother. We all laughed. To me it said a lot about Hannah Thompson's adjustment through the years. I looked up and saw a little poem on the wall. It read:

> Our lives are albums written through,
> With good or ill, 'false' and 'true,'

And, as the blessed angels turn
The pages of our years,
God grant they read the good with smiles
And blot the ill with tears.

*(Streams in the Desert)*

I left dear little Hannah Thompson, her faithful husband, Ted, and her fine Christian sons and their wives with smiles as I blotted my own tears.

# Her Excellency Masiofo Fetaui Mata'afa

wife of the PRIME MINISTER of WESTERN SAMOA

Many of the islands of the South Pacific give the appearance of having burst up out of the sea, some with mountains rearing up on a coral base formed from volcanic eruptions that pioneer missionaries described as "fire spewed out and kindled by the finger of God Himself." The mountain slopes dip into fertile valleys with rich forests and flat lands sloping gently toward the sea. The tropical climate is generally pleasant, but hurricanes can sweep across the islands with devastating fury.

In the tiny village of Mulinuu on the island of Western Samoa, Fetaui sat on a mat, legs crisscrossed. Nearby sat her three sisters and little brother. Outside, the rain came down with gale force. It was the Rainy Season.

It was on just such a day as this over a century before that John Paton's wife had died. The Christians on the islands were familiar with the story of John and Mary Ann Paton, missionaries to their islands.

Mary Ann Paton had been on the island less than three months before she died, but in that brief period of time she collected a class of eight women who came to her regularly to receive instruction. It was said of Mary Ann that she had about her a maturity of thought, a solidity of character, and a loftiness of aim and purpose. A resolution was passed by the missionaries on the island at the time of her death which read in part: "Her earnest Christian character, her devoted Missionary spirit, her excellent education, her kind and obliging disposition and the influence she was fast acquiring over the natives, excited expectations of great future usefulness." (The material quoted about John and Mary Ann Paton is from *John G. Paton: Missionary to the New Hebrides* and used by permission of The Banner of Truth Trust, London.)

Fetaui's parents were third generation Christians. Now she listened attentively as her mother once again told the story of how Christianity had come to the islands and to their family in particular. The story never ceased to thrill her.

"Your great-grandfather Petaia was a pastor, and your grandfather was a pastor. Christianity came to the islands with John Williams in 1830. He was a brave white missionary who later was killed by the pagans at Eromanga in the New Hebrides." Fetaui's thoughts took wings as her mother's voice trailed on.

In her mind she pictured what might have happened. Superstition and heathen rites had kept the people in bondage to a fear of the unknown God and led the islanders into dark and evil ceremonial exercises. They gloried in bloodshedding, tribal wars, and in cannibalism. They deified their chiefs and vainly tried to propitiate the Evil Spirits through incantations by their wizards and witches—the so-called sacred men and women. Slavish fear forced them into the most degrading and cruel practices. Fetaui was glad she hadn't been a little girl then!

The arrival of the missionary was greeted with suspicion and in some instances with killings; but persistent labors of love and acts of

135

kindness enabled the missionary to make inroads. The missionaries knew nothing of the language or the culture of the people, but they could smile, nod, and make signs to the islanders. Gradually the missionary's ears became familiar with the distinctive sounds of the language; and keenly alert, extraordinary progress was made in reducing their speech into written form. Fetaui knew this was where her great-grandfather had been helpful.

The first prayer offered in Samoa was a prayer of grace at a feast where these missionaries were being entertained. The prayer was said by a woman who was one of the party of John Williams. It was thought that this woman might have come from Tahiti or the Cook Islands, and the other islanders that accompanied John Williams as well. Fetaui wished she could have heard that prayer.

The very fact that the South Sea Islanders were ceaselessly groping after knowledge of the unknown God made it not as hard as might be supposed to gain their audience. Once their language and modes of thought were understood by the missionary, he was able to give them stories about the Jehovah God and his Son Jesus and the mighty works recorded in the Bible. Slowly the people responded, their interest aroused. Fetaui's great-grandfather was one such man. She was brought back from her reverie by her mother's voice: "Your great-grandfather didn't know any of the English language; yet he helped to translate the Bible into the best Samoan."

"But how did it happen?" one of the children asked the mother.

"In 1830 when John Williams landed he was met by the ruling King's orators. The King Malietoa was kindly disposed to this white man and gave him all the provisions he needed. The king had had a visionary talk with the woman Nafanua who told him that any more help he received for his people would have to come from above. And when John Williams came and said to the king, 'I have come to tell you of a greater King than you are,' the king asked the missionary to tell about this king. Then the missionary told King Malietoa about Jesus. After that the king turned to his followers and said, 'You will no more refer to me as Afioga (the title reserved for God), but from now on you will refer to me as Susuga (the title reserved for a lower chief). Today it is still the same.

"Yes," Fetaui's mother was saying, "your great-grandfather heard about this King—the real Afioga—and was inspired by the Holy Spirit to help translate the Bible."

The rain had ceased and the wind was no longer howling around their house. Fetaui's mother ended her story-telling. "It is time to get to work; the rain has stopped and the wind is no more blowing," she clapped her hands together. "Come, let us see the damage." The ground was strewn with half-ripe and wasted fruits. The children scampered to their duties.

Fetaui worked and thought. She was glad to hear about her great-grandfather—glad that the stone idols, charms, and sacred objects had been thrown away so long ago. It was good to be a Christian. She was only one year old when her grandfather had died, but she had been told that he had often said: "The strength of the family is based on its Christian heritage—what the ancestors had done." The blessings and opportunities which they enjoyed were not to be taken lightly. This she knew. Wasn't she soon to leave home and go to New Zealand and study at the government school? It was not a privilege granted to many. The possibility excited her.

Her Excellency, Fetaui Mata'afa, wife of the prime minister of Western Samoa, was sitting across from me. With flawless English she was relating some of the events of her life. She is a master speaker and we were enthralled. It was the fall of 1969, but at times I felt as though I was on the beautiful island of Samoa.

"In Samoa my father is a retired civil servant. We lived in a very unusual community, the traditional capital of our country. All the people who live there are the people who work for the government as civil servants. This traditional capital is also the burial place for all the royal leaders. It is where receptions are held for any important people from overseas. This is where my father worked as we grew up, and where we had a very interesting life as a family.

"My maternal grandparents were missionaries in Papua, New Guinea, an island north of Australia. It is still not all Christianized. Mother came here to Mulinuu as a nurse and married Dad. I am the eldest child and was born June 23, 1928. Mother died in 1942 when my brother was only two and a half. Dad worried about how he was going to raise his little ones, and he later remarried. There are three children in the second marriage, and all of us but one have had scholarships to New Zealand.

"In 1945 our government was beginning to think about independence, and New Zealand was interested in developing new island territories. They started what they called 'A Government Scholarship Scheme' in Western Samoa.

"The New Zealand Government had the responsibility of placing Samoan students wherever there was a vacancy. My sister and I went to Auckland, north of Wellington, which is the capital. We were at boarding school four years. After that I went on to teacher's training college and taught for one year. Then I went home.

"Because I was a scholarship student, I had to do what my government asked me to do. I had wanted to stay in New Zealand and do university work, but I had no choice, and in 1953 I found myself back in Samoa. From 1953 to 1961 I taught English, geography, and history at Samoa College, the only secondary school.

"I have been married since 1956. My husband is one of Samoa's royal sons. One doesn't go near them! But I had known him. His late mother and my mother became very great friends in the 1930s. They exchanged library books and were both fond of reading. My mother accompanied his mother to Fiji at one time. So in those days I would see this royal son. Since my husband is seven years older than I, I didn't speak to him. I had always known about him, but I don't think he knew about me.

"In 1953 we started a friendship, and soon thereafter he wanted to marry me. We were then married in 1956, and our wedding completely broke all Samoan tradition! He is the only present leader in Western Samoa; both of his parents are of royal ancestry, and so that means his wedding should have taken in the whole of Samoa. Instead we got married simply and quietly!

"Since we had decided we wanted to avoid fanfare, we went to the chaplaincy of the Apia Protestant Church. I wore a very simple white frock, carried a small bouquet, and had a short veil. After we said our vows, we went home, had a family dinner, and went off on our honeymoon. Samoan honeymoons are usually spent right where all the people are. We just got into his car, went off to a friend's house at the beach, very quietly. And oh, it was beautiful. This has characterized our marriage. We prefer to live simply and are thankful to God. I have seen many big weddings in Samoa that break up and are unhappy. There is a lot of exchange, even to this day, in fine mats and money between the wedding parties, in giving of materials and dowry. My husband was able to put his foot down. He is the only son. At the time we were married, he already held three titles."

Her new position as Her Excellency did not stand in the way of her doing what she had trained to do. Fetaui decided to continue teaching after they were married.

His Excellency took his bride to a beautiful home two miles from Apia. They have other houses in his other villages. But they are in the country and far from the capital, and so they continue to live in their original home.

Her husband spent five years in his country's theological college, and today his duties as prime minister of four main islands of Western Samoa keep him very active. The islands number about 135,000 population. Besides his political responsibilities he is Samoan chief with many villages that fall under his jurisdiction. Then as elder-deacon of their Congregational Church District he represents the laity from fifty churches.

As the wife of the representative of the laity, Her Excellency is expected to inspect all the pastors' manses once a year to see that they are well provided for because they have no set stipend.

The Samoan home is quite different from the typical American home. Fetaui smiles knowingly as she explains her duties. To us they may seem strange, but to the Samoan it is important. "In March every year I announce that I will be coming for inspection. I will inspect the linen, the crockery, mats, and other items. Our homes are not like yours. For the most part these homes do not have chairs. We sit on the floor, cross-legged on mats. We call our homes Fale. They are very open, with very little privacy. The art of changing one's clothes becomes quite a feat.

"Children in our homes behave very differently from children in this country too! We have one little girl, Naomi. In Samoan homes children are seen and not heard. I am training our daughter to be like that. Now she is in New Zealand attending school just as I, her mother, did. The child's duties in the home are to roll up the mats, take out the rubbish, fetch the firewood, fetch the water fresh from the spring; and when there are small ones in the family, they learn as early as eight and nine to nurse and care for the babies.

"The women cook over two big boulders with two bars across and fire in a small pit underneath."

In many of these respects the Samoan women are not so different from their ancestors. Yet, as I listened to this well-educated, attractively attired, intelligent woman, I knew the women of Samoa had come a long way since the days of John Paton and John Williams.

Education in Samoa has also come a long way. There are both pastor's schools and government schools. Fetaui herself is on a special committee investigating the possibilities of updating the Christian education in their church schools. Education is still not compulsory, but Fetaui feels that with the changes coming into the country from the outside that real strides will be made in improvement of education.

In November 1969 Her Excellency was asked to be the pro-chancellor of the University of the South Pacific in Suva, Fiji. This university is only about one year old and cares for the needs of the islanders of the South Pacific.

This is, indeed, a great honor for Fetaui Mata'afa. The king of Tonga is the chancellor. Fetaui's responsibility will be to chair the University Council's meetings. Of this she says, "Impartiality must be upheld at all times since the members of the Council are from various cultures and backgrounds."

As the wife of a recognized great man in the islands of Samoa, Her Excellency is able to exert a powerful influence for good. As president of the National Council of Women—the largest women's organization of all the islands—she has helped direct the building of a great community center in Apia. This is the chief town and seat of government for Western Samoa. People in this country may recognize it as the burial place for the famed Robert Louis Stevenson.

This community center will feature adult education classes, health and cultural services and provide a unique ministry to the islanders. There is a beautiful auditorium, a clinic, tea rooms, and even private rooms which are available for overnight sleeping accommodations to visitors on the island. The only paid employee is Mrs. Mata'afa's personal secretary; all other workers are volunteers. Her Excellency maintains an office in this community center where her many varied and important duties can be channeled into greatest effectiveness. In addition to the responsibilities already outlined, she is president of the Red Cross, very active in the Congregational Church Women's Fellowship, and president of the Pan-Pacific Southeast Asian Women's Association. In this latter capacity she strives to encourage friendly relations among the women in the islands. This is a non-governmental position which has branches around the world.

The work of United Church Women has strong appeal in the South Pacific, and Samoan women join with other women throughout the world in the yearly observance of Women's World Day of Prayer.

Fetaui Mata'afa explains such involvement by women on the island this way: "The women in Samoa are very active; so if you want something done in the church or in the government, it is the women that do the work. When the community center was being built, it was the women who hauled the rocks and the sand onto trucks and actually helped to erect the building."

Many years ago John Paton wrote in his diary, "Let those who lightly esteem their Bibles think on this—the poor converted savages gave the labour and proceeds of fifteen years to have the Word of God in their native tongue." This was brought to mind when Her Excellency underscored the meaningful place the Bible has in their lives. It is a meaning which has been passed down from one generation to another.

"We are brought up in the Christian faith, we grow into it, it is our way of life," she speaks with conviction. "In 1968 I was invited to speak in Birmingham, England, and I made this point: you had Christianity before us, and you have gone through the stage we are going through now—perhaps the European society has reached their peak, so called—you reach this materialistic tendency and you break away from what you have long believed. I hope we have learned through you from this that our Christian faith can mean more than that—that it will endure such testings. In Samoa the Christian way of life has been integrated into our own way of life and our national way of life. The authority of the chief has been transferred to the pastor, and the pastor has a tenacious hold on the people—they are expected to go to church, expected to have daily family worship. The church is so much a part of our people; it is not divorced from the state, and our constitution is based on Christian principles."

Her Excellency arose to leave. The interview was ended. But a friendship had just begun. His Excellency stood by her side; together they presented a picture of solidarity—tall, both of them well built, brown-skinned, and good looking. We embraced, kissed each other good-bye, and she said, "The Apostle Paul said it very well, 'There is neither Jew nor Greek, there is neither bond nor free, there is neither male nor female: for we are all one in Christ Jesus.' "

As I have reconstructed that interview and thought about Mrs. Fetaui Mata'afa over and over, I have been brought back to that which was said so many years ago about Mary Ann Paton—maturity of thought, solidity of character, loftiness of aim and purpose. Yes, the description fitted *this* twentieth-century Samoan leader among women who, with her husband, was giving to the islanders an example of Christlike living that could only inspire others to want to follow.

"Her earnest Christian character, her devoted missionary spirit, her excellent education, her kind and obliging disposition, and the

141

influence she was acquiring over the natives excited expectations of great future usefulness." Such were the words in tribute accorded Mary Ann Paton. Mary Ann herself would have said just such words about Fetaui! Yes, Mary Ann Paton's life was as seed sown that has borne fruit.

# Faith McCain Wells

### mother-in-law of SHERWOOD ELIOT WIRT

One day when Winola Wells Wirt was a child, she read in the Bible the words of Jesus, "O ye of little faith." She stopped right there. Imagine, she thought, the Bible speaking of her and her mother! For some time thereafter she went around hugging to herself this discovery. "O ye"—surely that meant her—"of little faith"—why, that was her mother's name. Wasn't her mother so small that she, Winola, couldn't even clop around in her shoes any more? The little girl sighed. Her feet were no longer size two and a half. And Mama's hands—they were so tiny that she had to go to the children's department in the store at nearby Elmira when she wanted to purchase gloves.

143

The time came when Winola finally shared with her mother her find in the Bible. Faith McCain Wells was quick to set the record straight!

The mother-in-law relationship has been made the brunt of jokes and derogatory comment since time immemorial. Rarely does one read or hear something to the contrary that places the wife's mother in a position of honor and respect. So it was that when I read that a certain minister had dedicated his first book to his mother-in-law, I decided to find out more about this lady. The search was a rewarding one.

Dr. Sherwood Eliot Wirt is the esteemed editor of the Billy Graham Evangelistic Association magazine *Decision,* now in five languages and seven editions with a circulation of over four million. He also has authored six books, and from his pen we are hopeful many more will be forthcoming. His best known writings include *Not Me, God; The Social Conscience of the Evangelical;* and *Passport to Life City (A Modern Pilgrim's Progress).* Dr. Wirt's life might have taken a far different course had it not been for his godly mother-in-law, small of stature but a devoted woman of faith and true to her name.

How did it come about? What was it that had so shaped and molded her that years later, after her death, her loved ones speak of her with gentle reverence?

Before Faith was born, her name had been chosen. Little Faith was a gentle soul. When four years old she was stricken with diphtheria during a tragic epidemic that descended on the little farming community. Each household buried its dead, frequently at night— so fearful was the populace of the dread disease. Antibiotics were four decades away, but there was God and the faith for which this child had been named. Her mother, Sarah, prayed, "And the prayer of faith shall save the sick" (James 5:15).

Suddenly there was a feeble movement in the crib. The little face seemed to come back to life, and the eyelids fluttered. From that moment Faith began to get well. Because her throat had been paralyzed, she had to relearn to swallow. Walking was a fresh adventure; but God had spared her life.

Throughout her youth the Old Testament was opened in the morning and the New Testament at night. Nothing was allowed to defer or interrupt the period of worship. There was a dignity and dependence upon God that left an indelible imprint upon the participants. In later years when her eyesight was failing, Faith McCain

Wells was able to quote Scripture from memory to a remarkable degree; and when her son-in-law, daughter, or grandson would start a verse, she would help them finish it. "Thy word have I hid in my heart!" (Ps. 119:11).

Faith's artistic sensibilities asserted themselves early in life. She had a feeling for beauty that would not be denied. By the time she reached school age, she was painting primitive but creditable oils on scraps of wood.

Faith's father, David, was convinced that his daughter possessed unusual ability. One night he walked in the door with an exciting prospect. He would barter milk and vegetables with a local artist in town; in return she would give Faith lessons in painting. Before long the art teacher recognized that Faith's gift required more advanced instruction. She had provided, however, a start for the artistically inclined farm girl who was daily adding fuel to the flame of ambition in her girlish heart.

Circumstances conspired to prevent Faith from finishing high school at the county seat. It became necessary for her to return to the farm, where she continued reading, painting, and helping with chores. "She was a lifelong student," recalls her son-in-law, "and while she had no row of diplomas to prove it, her breadth of knowledge amazed me."

For a while she lived with her sister in New York. During that time she received painting lessons from a well-known professional artist of the Hudson River School.

It was at the high school commencement exercises in nearby Turnerville that Faith McCain, while attending with a friend, saw for the first time the young man who tipped her heart. She was transfixed by the appearance of the second tenor in a quartet that sang that night. She was convinced he was the handsomest youth she had ever seen. Later when he stepped forward to receive his graduation diploma, a thrill went through her as the principal called out, "John Eppes Wells," and the blond young man came to the front of the platform. When he appeared to smile at Faith, she felt as if her heart had turned to syrup, for he looked directly at her and their eyes met and held for a long moment.

Three years passed before Faith and Eppes met. During all that time she cherished the hope that someday, somewhere, their paths might cross. Eventually they did, and romance began that summer.

Before he returned to college, Eppes and Faith had seen each other a few times and agreed to correspond. The letters they exchanged were models of propriety. It was months before they stopped calling each other "Miss" and "Mr." They exchanged poetry, quotations from the great essayists, hopes and aspirations, discussions about the Lord and his universe, and some of their deeper feelings.

Next summer Eppes and Faith saw each other occasionally, though not nearly often enough. Faith treasured every moment. She shared with her lover her "dreaming rock," a flat boulder on her father's property. There she took Eppes' letters to open and read in solitude.

After he had returned to school, a small package had arrived at the farm from Ohio, where Eppes was studying. Her heart pounding, Faith hurried out to "her" rock to open the package. As her fingers untied the wrappings she suspected it might be a jeweler's box. She touched the tiny fastener on the box and lifted the lid. Within gleamed a tiny but lovely diamond. The stationery folded around the box conveyed the loving thoughts that the sender would have liked to deliver in person.

In one of his letters Eppes wrote, "The standard greeting out here is, 'Nice day, ain't?' I am supposed to consider that the customer is always right, but the nicest day will be June 17th." The nicest day arrived and the wedding bells pealed. A lovely ceremony took place in Faith's family home. The honeymoon was a kaleidoscope of happy days. Eppes was an enthusiastic photographer, and Faith posed for his Brownie No. 1 camera everywhere they went. Eppes brought his bride to the thriving county seat of Towanda, Pennsylvania, where he had accepted a position as pharmacist.

As a talented young couple, the Wellses were welcomed into the social life of Towanda, where their activities revolved around the church. Each taught a Sunday school class, attended morning and evening services, and together they participated in Christian Endeavor. There were also prayer meetings, and Eppes was soon singing in a gospel quartet.

There were no forty-hour weeks in those days and no coffee breaks, but Eppes would dash up the hill twice a day for a brief "dinner" and "supper" with his beloved. Sometimes a nagging fear crept into Faith's mind. He did have a heart condition, and he was so active.

During the second year of their marriage Faith became pregnant. She was delighted, and so was Eppes. During the ensuing months Faith was called back to the farm on the hilltop because of her

146

mother's illness. She spent the time making baby clothes for the expected first child. The child was due in January but chose to appear early, on December 28. It was the coldest night of the year, thirty degrees below zero, and there were no telephones. Eppes performed a minor miracle by getting the doctor there in time.

Faith and Eppes named the infant "Helen Winola," the latter being the name of a well-known Indian princess in the region. After a difficult start, the baby thrived and became an added joy in the life of the young couple. A year later Eppes learned of a drugstore for sale in Tioga, Pennsylvania, near the New York state line. Eppes suspected that his hold on life was precarious and felt his family would have more security with an established business. After much prayer the move was made.

Then came a tragic day, just two months after Faith had given birth to twin daughters who died. John Eppes Wells succumbed to the heart condition that had haunted him most of his life. Baby Winola was just four years old. Little Winola was told, gently, that her father was in Heaven. It was a long time before she knew anything about the funeral and the burial or was taken to the cemetery plot.

With the courage that was to mark her long life, Faith took over the management of the pharmacy and sought to make a success of it. In the following years she sold the drugstore and moved to Tuckhannock, where she opened a specialty shop for which she was well suited. Her artistic skills lent themselves to this new venture. After her daughter graduated as high school valedictorian, Faith sent her to college and gave her the education of which she herself had been deprived. Later after a period of teaching, Winola joined her mother in the business, learning from her, traveling, ordering, and buying. On a summer trip following a semester at the University of Arizona, Winnie met the man who was to become her husband.

After their marriage Sherwood and Winola settled in California. He had been assigned to a student church in the country for weekend ministry while he was attending seminary. Faith left the cares of business life behind and moved from the East after a year, to join her daughter and newly acquired son-in-law on the West Coast.

The move was destined to have effects that she could not possibly foresee. Dr. Wirt explains what happens in this manner: "I was involved in seminary work. When mother moved into our home (or rather, we moved into hers, for she bought the house), she began to hold regular evening devotions as she had held them since the days when she lived with her parents. I had been in a seminary a year and had become quite sophisticated. I went to the seminary each morning to absorb all the latest critical teaching about the Bible, then returned home at night to be given the unadulterated Word of God by my mother-in-law. I was becoming a theological schizophrenic and didn't know what to believe. I didn't like the skeptical Bible teaching I was getting in the seminary, but it was so self-assured it was hard to imagine there was an alternative view. I didn't like what I was getting at home either, because it seemed to be based on an unintelligent approach to ancient history.

"Mother would dial Charles E. Fuller, Dr. M. R. DeHaan, and Percy Crawford on the radio every Sunday afternoon. When Harry Ironside came to town, she insisted I hear him. She was forever quoting from Donald Grey Barnhouse, Wilbur M. Smith, Arno Gaebelein, Reuben A. Torrey, and others. I reacted strongly to it all. I'd go back up the hill to the seminary where they had never heard of any of these people.

"Mother's view prevailed, because in spite of her theological limitations she had the truth, she had the Holy Spirit, and she had love. She would say to me: 'Sherwood, I'm not saying these things to you just to lecture you, I'm saying them because I love you.' Soon her teaching began to be reflected in my ministry, and I found myself proclaiming a more evangelical gospel. Other people helped, including my church folk. I remember kneeling down one night in my room and asking the Holy Spirit to come into my life. I was moving out deeper into the things of the Lord. By the time I graduated from seminary, many things straightened out. I had a lot of growing to do; I didn't have a clear understanding of the authority of the Scripture; I had a lot of questions and suspicions—but there was a change."

The years ahead were to effect the final change that resulted in the making of the man readers know today as the editor of *Decision*. When in 1958 Dr. Wirt wrote his first book on the Beatitudes, which was published as *The Cross on the Mountain* and then as *Magnificent Promise,* the dedication read:

To FAITH McCAIN WELLS

who showed me His face

Faith McCain Wells' ambition was not to achieve earthly fame. She took small credit for her artistic gifts, saying they were from

148

the Lord and she deserved no praise for developing talents he had given her. Yet in her quiet way she etched for herself a lasting place in the minds and hearts of many with whom she came into contact. Winola Wells Wirt, now an author in her own right (*Interludes in a Woman's Day, Of All Places*), has written of her mother:

"Her hands were not the delicate, helpless hands one might associate with the lack of size. They were sturdy, squarish, barely able to reach an octave, yet so skilled on piano and organ. They were hands that carried coal scuttles and wielded the most delicate brush strokes on paintings; hands that held a healing touch for a child's feverish forehead, or gave forth efficient spats to that same child if she were naughty; hands that could prepare gourmet foods or design enchanting millinery; hands that could balance books and accounts or write poetry; hands that could turn unerringly to beloved passages in the Bible."

And we could add—hands whose most important function in later years were to be clasped in fervent prayer as she interceded for her son-in-law—this man in whom she saw greatness that God could bless and use to enrich the lives of others through the printed page in a far-reaching ministry.

In February, 1961, Faith McCain Wells went to be with her Lord, going as gently as she had lived.

# Maude E. Smith

mother of "CHUCK" SMITH

Her head rested quietly on the pillow and her hands were folded. Her body which had been racked by pain now relaxed peacefully. Her eyes were closed, but she wasn't asleep. "Son," she called weakly, and her son responded at once.

She opened her eyes and reached out her hands to clasp his. "Son, I want to tell you good-bye and I want to tell you what a marvelous husband you've been."

Her son, Charles, leaned close and said, "Mom, aren't you sort of mixed up? I'm your son."

"Yes, yes, I know Charles," she replied. "But I've watched you

150

as a husband, and I just want you to know that you're a marvelous husband and a marvelous son. Keep following the Lord, son. Keep serving him, Charles . . ." Her voice trailed off.

Charles Smith leaned closer and whispered, "Mom, come on mom, things are going to be fine. You're going to be great."

The eyes fluttered open again, and she looked at him with eyes of love and whispered, "No . . . I'm telling you good-bye, son." That day Maude Smith went into a coma, and three days later went to be with the Lord.

It had been a year before that she'd first evidenced discomfort and pain necessitating hospitalization. At that time her condition was diagnosed as cancer. Her son recalls her words and the deep faith she evidenced in the hours preceding the operation. "My life is in God's hands. Whatever the Lord sees fit to do, that's what I want, too. After all, Charles, your father and brother are on the other side and I have pullings in that direction, too." Her confidence in God was unshakable. "She exuded trust in the Lord. It was really tremendous," says her son.

Following the operation she had what appeared to be a good recovery. When her son Paul and his wife were needed in South America on a missionary assistance program, she wanted to stay with their children. But, during their absence, she once again became ill. For six months she lived in constant pain and suffering; yet, her children recall that there was never a word of complaint—they could walk into her sick room and her hands would be raised in worship, praising God, talking to him.

She moved to Charles' home, and it became an overwhelming experience for him. "She was a terrific domestic—baking pies, cookies, rolls, cake, all the things I enjoy. She ministered constantly to the needs of others. Her dedication to Christ showed in her dedication to her family. So many times in our growing-up years when my brothers and I would be arguing over a piece of pie, rather than eat her own, she'd give her piece to us to divide. When I'd walk into her room and see her body and her condition, I'd look at those hands which had ministered to our needs through the years—how in sickness I'd feel the comfort of her hands on my forehead, things of this nature—and this one particular day as she lay suffering, I reached for her Bible. It opened to Isaiah 35. As I read it, I received such comfort and assurance from the Lord.

"Another time, early one morning, I walked in to check on her. As I knelt there by her bed, I found myself praying, 'Father, if you want to take my mother, I don't have any hold on her. I'm not going to demand that you heal her; but Lord, I don't see why she should have to suffer. It's been six months since she's had any sound sleep. Take her Lord, if this is your will; and I won't grieve over her parting knowing that she is with you. But if you don't take her now, Lord, if just for a moment, for a little while, if it's possible I would be willing, I would be glad to take her suffering. Just move it over on me, Lord, for a little while and give her some relief.' " As he prayed, Charles Smith says he felt the presence of Christ more close and real than he's ever felt in his entire life.

"It was like Christ was standing there saying, 'Charles, that's a very foolish thing, for I bore her suffering for her.' And at that very moment my mother sighed and said, 'Praise the Lord. This is the first time I've felt free from pain in six months. This is wonderful.' "

In the next two days Maude Smith rallied and slept. She'd wake up praising and thanking the Lord for taking away the pain. And then God took her to himself.

The Christian way of death. Pleasant? No, but triumphant for the Christian. Maude Smith knew she was going to die; yet, she could look beyond the certainty of dying to the even more real certainty of heaven. She called it "Home." She looked beyond the corridors of this life to eternity and being at home with God. Most people are frightened by the mere word "death," but not Maude Smith. She exemplifies that one who can say with the Apostle Paul, "For to me to live is Christ, and to die is gain" (Phil. 1:21).

When God calls home a tired soul,
And stills a fitful breath,
Love Divine is waiting there,
This, too, is birth not death.

But living for Maude Smith did mean Christ.

When God sends forth a spotless soul,
To learn the ways of earth,
A Mother's love is waiting here,
We call this wonder birth.

Physical birth. Maude E. Ward came into this world on October 22, 1902. She grew up in trying and adverse circumstances, but somehow her Mother held the family of three girls and two boys together. Maude's father had "gold fever" and left his family in search of the illusive stuff. He never returned. The family was uprooted frequently but finally settled in Santa Barbara, California.

Maude was an ambitious and intelligent young girl and graduated from high school at sixteen. Her first job took her to the Arbuckle Movie Studio where she was noticed by Randolf Hearst who asked her to go to New York and appear on stage. It was no wonder! She was a very lovely dark-haired, dark-eyed beauty, with a flawless complexion and a dazzling smile. She took some screen tests, but when she saw the type of life the stars were living, Maude decided she didn't want any part of it. She turned her attention to preparing herself for a stenographic position.

When Charles H. Smith went to the Southern Counties Gas Company to complain about a bill, he discovered, in his words, "the most beautiful girl he'd ever seen." He forgot all about complaining, but paid the bill, and obtained his first date with the beautiful Maude Ward who was working as a secretary!

When she was chosen beauty queen of the Santa Barbara Fiesta Days, Charles Smith jealously followed the float she was riding on all the way down State Street in his model "T" Ford. It didn't take him long to ask his "Princess," as he lovingly called her, to marry him.

Charles Smith had a tremendous personality. He was very dynamic and outgoing. His father was the vice president of the Southern Pacific Railway, and Charles grew up in relative luxury. He and his three brothers attended military schools as boys, and all four were commissioned as chief petty officers in the navy at the time of World War I. The family home was in Philadelphia, and they owned a beach home in Atlantic City, New Jersey. Later they moved to Santa Barbara, California.

Charles had been raised in boarding schools and was the epitome of a gentleman. Of course, Maude was swept off her feet by the graciousness and charm of this man who was ten years older than she and they were married.

Maude was the practical one, Charles the romantic. She had some adjustments to make in the early years of their marriage. They moved to Tuscon, Arizona, then back to Santa Barbara, and on to Ventura, California.

Their first child, a daughter, was born. Now it was Charles who was working as a salesman for the Southern Counties Gas Company. They were a church-oriented family but were not living dynamic Christian lives. Charles was an elder, Sunday school superintendent, boy scout leader, and active member in the sheriff's reserve. His busyness revealed an inner emptiness—a searching for something. Maude, however, began looking for help and wandered into a tent revival. At the close of the meeting she confessed her need for Christ to fill the vacuum in her heart. This conversion experience so disturbed her husband that he sought to close down the tent meeting; instead, he, too, found the reality of a Living Christ.

At this time their daughter, Virginia, became violently ill. A cousin had just died of spinal meningitis; and when Virginia went into convulsions, Maude was sure she was dying. A nurse, living in the same building, told Mrs. Smith to get the child to the doctor immediately. Instead, Maude ran next door to the church parsonage. The minister came over, saw the child and the distraught young mother, and told her to get her eyes off the child and just pray to the Lord.

Maude dropped to her knees and prayed: "Oh Lord, I know you are able to do anything; you are able to give my child back to me restored in health. I vow that if you heal this child, I will rededicate my life to you for whatever ministry you might have for me and my unborn child." Yes, Maude was carrying another baby.

Charles rushed in and found Maude praying. He dropped to his knees beside her joining in pleading with God to spare their daughter. It revolutionized their lives. Today Virginia is alive, well, and joyously living for the Lord in Modesto, California, with her family.

This was followed by living lives of faith, totally dependent upon God.

Charles became involved in a jail ministry. On weekends they would have prisoners in their home, setting up cots in the garage, serving meals, and giving them the gospel message. Sunday school, morning worship, Wednesday night prayer meetings, revivals, and Daily Vacation Bible School all became a part of their normal activities.

Maude and Charles were overjoyed when Charles, Jr., was born. The father went around telling his friends, "Praise the Lord, it's a boy!" He was to repeat that phrase two additional times in the following years when son Paul and son Bill were born.

At Big Sisters Hospital in Ventura, when Maude's infant son was placed in her arms for the first time on June 25, 1927, she cradled him tenderly, and then said, "My boy, I promised to give God my life and to dedicate myself to his ministry." Then she raised her eyes heavenward and prayed, "And God, I will fulfill to you my promise and hereby vow in this son that you have given me to do that which I said I would do."

Her son—lovingly called "Chuck" now by all who know him—relates what happened as a result of that vow. "From my earliest years, from the time I was first able to comprehend, she started having me memorize Scriptures. She would follow me around the yard even as I would be swinging or playing, repeating Scriptures to me and having me say them back to her.

"And then she started to teach me how to read, and the book she used was the Bible. Actually I learned how to read out of the Bible when I was four years old. I remember her telling of my reading to her—I would come to some of the difficult names that I couldn't pronounce and would spell them out. And when I couldn't even spell them out I'd say, 'Mother, what is a tent upside down?' trying to describe the letters because I didn't know the complete alphabet at the time.

"But always I was surrounded by love and prayer. I cannot, in my early childhood, remember ever going to sleep at night but what the last thing I heard before I fell asleep was my mother praying or reading the Bible out loud in the living room. I remember awaking in the morning, and the first thing I'd hear was mother praying out loud. She was a woman of prayer and the Word—just a beautiful fellowship with God constantly."

Son Paul remembers vividly, "Mother would relate Bible stories to us while she was ironing. We always had a family altar and Bible reading."

Virginia recalls the music lessons and how they grew up with an appreciation for good music. "Chuck was youth leader for our young people's groups at church and was very popular. He was well endowed with good looks, intelligence, and a charming personality. But more important, he was responsible.

"He knew how to work and he knew the value of money. I remember when Chuck was fourteen and our father became ill. It was Christmastime, and if it hadn't been for Chuck and his paper route, we'd have had no gifts."

No generation gap existed, nor were the children in the Smith family rebellious. Maude and Charles let their children know that they were being trusted. This engendered within the children the desire to live up to their parents' expectations. When Chuck started dating, Maude worried about her handsome elder son. He was a "charmer" and girls just naturally "fell" for him. Her sister laughingly "tells" on him: "He was in and out of love so many times we doubted if he'd know the real thing when it came along. But when he met Kay we all recognized that Chuck did know true love."

But he might have had mistaken judgment had it not been for Maude's gentle guidance. She would say when he'd bring home girls to meet the family, "Well now, Charles, do you really feel that this girl would be all that you need and want as a life-long partner?" Then, very carefully, she would point out some of the girl's character that he hadn't noticed.

Maude's husband was a successful salesman in his work, but his children are more convinced that he was more thrilled at "selling" Jesus than doing anything else. But Maude contributed to this, too. She and her husband prayed together every day before he left for work. Then, at day's end, they would rejoice together in answered prayer as he related how he had been used by God to lead someone to Christ.

Maude Smith was an intercessor. Each detail of her life, those of her family, and the needs of others were committed to the Lord in prayer. Paul says, "The need for mom's prayers seemed as necessary as gas and oil for our car. Throughout our lives it was just the most natural thing to stop with mom to have a little prayer for our protection before we left for school, on dates, to athletic contests, etc."

Her daughter adds, "When we would come up on her praying, you could feel the presence of God that surrounded her, and her face would be aglow. Sometimes you felt like you were standing on holy ground."

She was a loving mom—always keeping a well supplied cookie jar and the children's clothes mended; she fed her family balanced meals and taught them how to care for their physical needs. They were given a consistent and gracious example in the home of the Christian life and conduct.

The Smith family moved to Santa Ana, California, when Chuck was in high school. Maude had never told him that she'd dedicated him to the ministry. He says, "I don't think she wanted me to be influenced by something like this. She wanted it to come strictly from within. And so, when I would talk of becoming a doctor (and I was taking the courses that would lead to a medical profession), she never said a thing.

"Then one summer I went to camp. There I was really moved by the Holy Spirit to a full dedication of myself to Christ and felt very definitely the call of God to go into the ministry.

"I came home and announced this to my mother. Tears filled her eyes, but it was not until ten years later that she sat down with me and shared how she had dedicated me for the ministry. But she waited all those years to make certain I knew that this was God's leading."

Charles Smith, Jr., went on into Bible college after high school, finished his education, married in June 1948, and then went into the pastorate. Paul Smith, likewise, went into full-time Christian service. Maude and her husband had a keen interest in the ministries of their sons. The years moved along.

It was in 1959 that her youngest son, Bill, and her husband were killed in an airplane crash. Bill had a private plane and was flying it. He and his father were returning from San Diego in a storm and crashed on the Camp Pendleton base.

Maude's faith never wavered, and even before she received official notification, she told Chuck, "God has spoken to me in prayer. 'The Lord has given and he has taken away. Blessed be the name of the Lord.' I know they are with the Lord now." A few hours later the CAP called to say they'd found the plane and that there were no survivors.

It was Maude's brave example that made the loss easier for her children to bear. She didn't indulge in self-pity but bravely set about to make a new life for herself. It was to her that her children turned even though hers was by far the greater loss—having lost her sweetheart and companion and youngest son (he was twenty-four and unmarried). All of this happened on a Saturday; yet, the next day Chuck was in his accustomed place in the pulpit preaching, witnessing to God's love and faithfulness. And Maude? She was sitting right there, facing the tragedy fearlessly, demonstrating her trust in the Lord.

There were pastorates in Prescott and Tucson, Arizona, for Chuck and his lovely wife, Kay. Then they pastored in Corona and Huntington Beach and finally were led to Costa Mesa, California.

The work at Calvary Chapel, which has now become known around the world as "America's most unusual church" and was featured in *Look* magazine, 9 February 1970, was down to about twenty-five members when Chuck Smith felt led of God to undertake the work there. His parishioners were stable "establishment-type" people, and the work was growing. But one evening, as Chuck and Kay met with some of their people, the subject of the drug problem among young people came up. The conversation centered upon the needs of the kids who were its victims. They all had to admit the problem existed and was growing. What's more, it was right there in their own backyard!

"We determined that we should seek somehow to reach these young people with the gospel of Jesus Christ," he states.

The pattern—born out of seeing his mother seeking the Lord's will and way—was set in motion once again by Maude Smith's son as he prayed, asking the Lord for a method to reach the kids.

"The idea was given that we should open up a Christian communal house to let the kids come in and live. It would be open twenty-four hours a day for those that needed help, for those who were on drugs and wanted to come down, or for whatever the needs were. We extended a hand to the young people through this house. We had a young couple who volunteered to staff it.

"Soon we outgrew this two-bedroom house in Costa Mesa and had to get a larger place. Within a week we had twenty young people living in the house, sleeping on the floors, in the hallways and kitchen.

"From this house there sprang up a second house in Riverside, then a third in Fontana, one in Phoenix, Arizona, and then in Corona. A group of ministers came down from Oregon and told of the tremendous need up there because drugs were so heavy around the university in Eugene. We told the kids about it, and sixty-five of them volunteered to go.

"Then houses opened in Newport Beach, Garden Grove, Huntington Beach, and Buena Park. We staff the houses with married Christian couples.

"We had outgrown our church facilities, as the kids from our communal houses would fill the services to overflowing. They were telling others who weren't even living in the houses. We acquired our present church property in a miraculous way and built an auditorium to seat 250 people. The first Sunday we had 300! We put up tents, went into double services, then triple services, added onto the building, and still do not have enough room." (Soon a new facility will be built, at the time of this writing.)

As he related this to me, Chuck Smith's face radiated with joy. It registered the humility of a man deeply committed to knowing and following the will of the Lord. And through it all, there was this

ever present feeling that to Chuck Smith there would never cease to be amazement, a standing in awe, as it were, that God should allow him to be in this work.

They're called hippies by the world. But when they come to Calvary they become "Jesus People." In their colorful garb, with bare feet, long hair, and beards they are welcomed and loved. Chuck says, "There is so much love and acceptance both from the kids and from the adults that I've never been around a place where there is more love manifested and you can feel it."

And indeed you can! The first time I walked into Calvary, I left stating, "You can just feel love bouncing off the walls."

Eleven acres have been acquired and the church must, of necessity, expand its facilities. They minister to thousands every night of the week with Bible studies that have the kids overflowing out of the church, sitting on benches and the sidewalk and grounds outside the building. There are triple morning services and one again on Sunday evenings. At every service scores accept Jesus Christ as Savior.

A baptism on the beach at Corona Del Mar in May 1971 witnessed over one thousand young people giving evidence of their newly found love for Jesus. Documentary films were made by BBC (British Broadcasting Corporation) and ABC (American Broadcasting Corporation).

How does one explain a ministry like that? Chuck Smith will tell you it is because of prayer and love. It is because the Bible is being taught and honored.

"I tried for years to be an evangelist," he says. "I wanted to be dynamic, powerful, and persuasive. My ministry was nothing. And then God spoke to my heart and said 'I called you to teach.' I decided right then to teach people rather than to preach to them. God began to start these people growing in their knowledge of the Word to where they became the evangelists. From that time on the ministry began to expand and mushroom. The Scripture that God gave to me was: 'And he gave some to be apostles; and some, prophets; and some, evangelists; and some, pastors and teachers. For the perfecting of the saints for the work of the ministry, for the edifying of the body of Christ.'

"When I started being just what God had called me to be—a teacher—then God began to bring in the others that caused the body to grow."

It is a work that will continue to grow as the Bible is faithfully

159

upheld week after week. It's the same Word that transformed the life of young Maude Smith. It's the same Word she faithfully instilled into her children that is now bearing fruit in thousands who respond as her son gives it out.

Chuck Smith today in appearance is a very ordinary man (balding with a dark fringe of black curly hair, the father of four children) possessed with extraordinary love, patience, and understanding. He has a powerful voice which conveys the Truth in a compelling way. He seems to have a perpetual smile on his face which comes through in his speech. His sister says she thinks he was born smiling. But the "hungering and thirsting" are being fed. This is New Testament Christianity in action. At Calvary the cultural gap is being bridged through a fellowship of love.

Where does a man acquire that kind of love? Chuck Smith saw it in his mother first. What a responsibility this places upon the mothers of the world! He says, "I feel that I have the most fantastic heritage in all the world because of my mother and father. She was sold out completely for Jesus Christ and lived a consistent Christian life before us. This explains why my ministry is what it is."

There's a tombstone in Fairhaven Cemetery in Santa Ana, California, and an inscription engraved on it that reads: "Jesus Never Fails." You'll see there also the name Maude E. Smith, for this was the theme of this woman's life.

# Jane Hill

### wife of EDWARD HILL

She wrapped herself in the draperies and dreamed her favorite dream. It was nighttime, eight o'clock to be exact. The huge back-yard was ablaze with lights, and guests were seated all around. The yard had never looked lovelier. Flowers were blooming everywhere, a riot of gorgeous color, their fragrance filling the night air. And in the far corner a large clump of pampas grass, with its white plumes looking like cotton candy swaying ever so slightly in the evening stillness, provided the perfect backdrop for the wedding which was underway.

It was such a beautiful dream—a dream she never tired of

dreaming. Every detail was etched in her thinking except one—the face of the man she'd marry. What would he look like? Who would he be? What would be his name?

And now she was hearing the words: I, Edward Hill, take thee Jane Coruthers. . . . Suddenly she roused and shook her head. But this was no dream. She looked down at her lovely white gown, around at the smiling sea of faces, and up into the handsome face of the tall man beside her. Her dream had become reality! This was her wedding night. Every detail was just as she'd always dreamed it would be except that the dream man, who before was always faceless, was standing beside her smiling down at her with tender love. It was a face she'd come to love. It was over—she was now Mrs. Edward Hill.

She looked again at the pampas grass—it had always been her favorite spot, and God had performed a miracle just a few hours before. Ever since she was a little girl, she knew she wanted to be married right there where she'd spent so many happy hours. It was a beloved place. How many times had she wrapped herself in her mother's draperies pretending they were her wedding gown? She wondered. But up until four o'clock on that August day in 1955 it was doubtful that the pampas grass or any of the flowers would be in bloom. It had been a dry year in Prairie View, Texas, and even though her father, Professor Coruthers, was in charge of the Agricultural-Economics Department of Prairie View College, no amount of coaxing and care on his part could make the flowers bloom for Jane's wedding unless there was some rain.

And then it began to rain—just hours before the wedding. A hard pouring down rain. Would it stop before the wedding was due to begin? Would she have to be married in the college auditorium?

God, who loves his children and delights to give them good and happy gifts, was going to prove himself in a wonderful way to this special child of his. Today, Jane Hill says, "It was as though he really gave his sanction to our wedding in a special way. Just before the sun would ordinarily go down, the rain stopped and the sun burst out scorching hot. The combination of rain and heat made every flower burst into full bloom and the yard never looked more beautiful."

Quite in contrast, ten years later Jane Hill would stand beside her husband watching the south central area of Los Angeles, California, where they lived become a blazing torch as an eruption of holocaust proportions took place. In the years following their marri-

162

age Edward and Jane Hill had led a fairly peaceful life. But Watts and the 1965 riots were something else.

For the peace-loving, gentle Jane Hill, wanton destruction, arson, looting, and violence came as unwelcome invaders, alien to her nature. Yet, they showed her the need for joining with her husband in his efforts to establish a headquarters for coordinating and carrying on a campaign to saturate the Negro community with the message of Jesus Christ. Thus it is that the World Christian Training Center stands in the heart of the inner city pointing the way—one way—to Jesus Christ who alone can unite ethnic groups and bring peace and stability to a community through individually changed lives.

Jane Hill's background did not especially qualify her for the role she fulfills as wife of a much sought-after speaker and leader. Born October 20, 1934, in Pine Bluff, Arkansas, to John and Susie Coruthers, Jane lived a very sheltered life. Her father was in charge of the Agricultural Experiment Farm of Arkansas State College, later moving to Prairie View College, in Prairie View, Texas, where she lived until marriage.

Her father was known as an eminent educator. Both parents were professional people. She grew up in a cultural situation on a college campus. Her dignity, social upbringing, and refinement are immediately evident as one converses with her. This was in stark contrast to the more deprived background of her husband. But in this regard she has been tremendous help to him, bridging the gap as it were for Edward Hill whose own childhood lacked distinctive social amenities.

Jane had dreams of being a nurse—dreams which her parents did not necessarily prefer. In high school she became national vice-president of the new Homemakers of America Organization qualifying herself for a four-year scholarship in home economics. But Jane disqualified herself by direct choice. She explains: "I was at the national convention and knew they were going to offer me this scholarship. I didn't feel I should take it and deprive someone else because I knew I wanted to be a nurse. I was alone in the dormitory where we were quartered, and I just prayed to God, turning my life over to him, and asked that his will would be done in my life. I asked him to be my Savior and my Lord."

She first met Edward Hill while in high school, and he was in Prairie View College. He was dynamic and popular. He was talkative. At first she wondered if he was too outgoing. As they became

163

better acquainted, Jane discovered this was just his personality and she began to appreciate him for what she truly found him to be— warm, sincere, genuine.

A very shy, unassuming girl, Jane found herself drawn to him, respecting him and his leadership qualities. Edward Hill, however, saw in the quiet Jane Coruthers a very intelligent young woman, vitally interested in others. "She needed me. My wife has an unusual ability to hide her intelligence. She made me feel that if I didn't go to her rescue, this poor, little defenseless girl would be out all by herself. Yet, the truth is she has a master's degree with almost all A's and is most capable. But I was attracted to her, recognizing great inner qualities, and she became a tremendous fan and supporter of me. And I needed that. She's always been full of encouragement, saying sweet things, just fulfilling a part of me that needed to be treated that way."

As Edward Hill observed the Coruthers family, he saw a family unity that was delightful and beautiful. Jane was a product of harmonious family living. He knew a woman with a background like that could be a great asset to him as he envisioned his own future.

"She looks like a queen," he thought, "but more, she acts like one." It was true. Jane had a regal bearing. She was not haughty but was ever so sweet with a totally innocent demeanor. Edward courted her gallantly for four and a half years, but not before every member of the family had checked him out first. "I'll never forget our first date," he says smiling. "Professor Coruthers escorted the two of us to a concert and sat between us in the concert!"

Jane became "his baby"—a term of endearment Edward Hill uses to this day.

Edward undertook to help Jane in her spiritual growth and development. He was a young preacher whose messages made living the Christian life very real and personal. Tuesday night prayer meetings on campus were a highlight of the week for Jane with Edward leading the discussions.

He showed her how to study the Bible. And he was always available to answer the many questions she plied him with. Jane wanted to become a member of the church he was pastoring, and she wanted him to baptize her. Wisely, however, Edward said no. "Jane, I don't want to ever feel that you are doing this because of your love for me. I want you to do this because of your love for

164

Jesus Christ. It cannot be a matter of personal persuasion because of our relationship. It must be real between you and Christ."

Jane accepted this and loved him all the more because of it. She waited. In her heart she knew she had really accepted Christ, but she was willing to wait to make certain Edward's doubts as to her reasons were really erased. Then one morning, without his knowing it, she came into his Sunday morning church service and walked down the aisle when the invitation was given; they both knew it was real and he baptized her.

Two months later they were married. The entire administration, faculty, and their families turned out for the happy event, in addition to the church members from Edward's pastorate in Houston. The popular "boy preacher" had quite a following.

The first night of their marriage Edward Hill took his bride to the new little home he had bought near the Mount Corinth Missionary Baptist Church. Jane had never seen the home, but trusted his judgment implicitly and found it to be a dream nest. In the years that followed she would move into two additional homes he had chosen without her presence. She says, "If he picks it, I like it and it's just exactly what I'd have chosen."

Jane became head nurse of one of the Houston hospitals and worked a three to eleven shift in the evenings for a time after their marriage. She had some apprehensions about assuming the role of minister's wife and wondered how she would fit in. Edward reassured her, stating that she was his wife, not the church's wife. She knew most of the church members probably knew a great deal more about church life and the Bible than she did, but her willingness to learn and her sweet ways endeared her to everyone, and she encountered no problems.

When baby Norva Rose was born, Edward and Jane rejoiced. Later, Edward Hill II blessed the family scene.

Jane continued to stay in the background, preferring her mothering responsibilities to involvement in outside activities. In 1961 her husband accepted the pastorate of Mount Zion Missionary Baptist Church in Los Angeles. This was a far different situation than pastoring the Houston church. Edward Hill found it a challenge. Jane stood by praying.

The church's very existence was at stake. It was snarled in quarrels and lawsuits. Members had lost heart. With characteristic determination and vision Edward Hill sought the Lord's guidance and then set to work to lead the people into becoming a strong church, "Bible-regulated, Christ-centered, and prayer-powered." God honored.

In 1966 when Campus Crusade was invited to the church to conduct lay institute meetings, Jane attended. She had been so busy pushing her husband ahead, seeing to it that he was dressed handsomely, that his clothes were clean, meals prepared, and the home kept neat that she had neglected involvement in sharing Christ with other people. The awareness jolted her. "I recognized there was something I was not doing. I knew there was something missing in my experience but wasn't exactly sure what it was. I discovered that we are each responsible for sharing Christ with other people. I then attended a week-long institute at Campus Crusade headquarters where I learned how to share Christ with others and discovered that we are saved to serve to help save other people. I recognized that it wasn't by any merits of our own that we are saved, but that it's a gift of God meant to be shared. I saw that I have a ministry of my own, not necessarily because of being a minister's wife, but because I am responsible to Christ.

"The most important thing in the world one can do is to teach others about Jesus Christ. When my husband had the dream about beginning the World Christian Training Center, I could share it with new joy." This she does with great zeal and love, serving on the staff teaching others what she has learned.

This was the missing link in Jane Hill's life. "Before I was worshiping God, I served him, I was a Christian, I believed in him, I let him lead my life as far as my daily routine at home, but I was too confined to my family. Now I've seen that I can be more helpful to my husband and of greater service to the Lord as I reach out to share Christ."

The south central area of Los Angeles is populated by over 450,000 people (at the time of this writing). Ninety percent of these are Negro. It has been described as a place of "operation frustration." The possibility of other riots, even more disastrous than the first, still looms on the horizon. But if people like Edward and Jane Hill can help it, the community will be reached for Jesus Christ instead.

The World Christian Training Center unapologetically admits that the strategy they employ is much like that which political candidates use to carry on successful campaigns. Jane Hill is enthusiastic in her support of the work being carried on there. She, along with her husband and others doing the training and recruiting of individuals, sees this as an opportunity to get a soul-winner in every block to take that block for Jesus Christ. "This is our aim," she explains.

To accomplish this, trainees, coming to the Training Center from all over, biweekly attend evening classes where they study six subjects: "Who is Jesus Christ?" "How to Receive Jesus Christ," "How to Lead Others to Christ," "How to Reach Your Block for Christ," "How to Turn Your Church to Soul Winning," and "How to Reach Your Family for Christ."

Thus, acting as "campaign headquarters for Jesus," the vision of Edward and Jane Hill is working in practical ways as white and black evangelicals are being trained to saturate their communities with the healing power of Jesus Christ. This is resulting in greater social justice, the salvation of souls, and an awakening of the laity in churches to obey the biblical commands.

In more recent years invitations for Jane to speak at various places across the nation have been forthcoming. Jane, who always thought she could never get up and stand in front of a group and talk, has discovered that in a very natural way she can now do this —teaching others about Christ and just letting her love for him overflow. "God can do it through me or anyone, and it's so wonderful to feel you are in the center of his will," she says glowingly.

She feels that the family unit is the most important unit that God seeks to work through. Because of her husband's busy schedule, much speaking, and being gone from home for weeks and months at a time, she devotes extra time to this responsibility of being both mother and daddy at such times. "This is how I can best help my husband, giving him the assurance he needs that in his absence his family is not being neglected spiritually as well as physically. The only point where I feel there is a place for me in the forefront of the ministry is when it relates to teaching about Jesus Christ and helping people to receive him. Other than that I am very content to stay in the background."

Mount Zion Missionary Baptist Church, in the heart of the troubled Los Angeles area, has a verse that has charted its course for the past ten years. It reads: "If you have the faith, God has the power."

Jane Hill typifies that Christian woman who knows the truth of standing on the promises of God, awake to every opportunity for Christ. As wife of the pastor of that church, she is making a great

167

contribution. Of her, Edward Hill says, "My wife's greatest asset is that her interest is in people and not things—she is totally void of things. Her love for the Lord spills over in her concern for and love for people."

As one of the outstanding black evangelical statesmen of this country, Edward Hill needs a woman like Jane Hill standing behind him. God in his infinite wisdom has provided her as the helpmeet for him.

## Nameless, but Known

An unknown writer penned these lines which present a thought-provoking truth:

> Life is a book in volumes three,
> The past, the present, the yet to be.
> The first is finished and laid away,
> The second we're writing day by day.
> But the third and last of the volumes three
> Is locked from sight; God keeps the key!

We are all authors, as it were, writing the story of our lives. But the most important chapter comes at that point where God is able to write our names in his Book of Life.

There are many references to this in the Bible. Moses was told, "Whosoever hath sinned against me, him will I blot out of my book" (Exodus 32:33). In the book of Daniel we read of the anguish and suffering the Jews are to experience, and then it says: "And yet every one of your people whose names are written in the Book will endure it" (12:1).

Paul, writing in Philippians 4:3, calls to remembrance those women who "worked side by side" with him "in telling the Good News to others." He speaks of them as "fellow workers whose names are written in the Book of Life." In the book of Revelation we are told "that everyone who conquers will be clothed in white, and their names will not be erased from the Book of Life." And Jesus himself said, "Rejoice, because your names are written in heaven" (Luke 10:20).

One day each of us shall hear the last words, "It is finished." The Scribe of years will have placed the last period after the last word. What is written will remain an indelible record. No year, month, day, hour, or minute can be recalled or relived. We shall be stripped of everything save what we are. Only one word will matter then—God's word. How happy we shall be if we hear him speak, "Well done, thou good and faithful servant; enter thou into the joy of thy Lord."

In the lives of these Silhouettes, you have seen God at work. God is in the business of transforming individuals into the likeness of his Son. You are nameless to me, but you are known to God and you are precious to him. The Bible says that Jesus is the author and finisher of our faith (Hebrews 12:2). Jesus waits at the door of every human spirit until he is either turned away or invited in. Jesus paid the penalty for mankind's sins when he died on the cross, and he becomes the Savior of each person who trusts him.

Billy Graham has said that you are not prepared to live and face the problems of life until you are ready to die. If you have never done so, dear reader, trust Jesus Christ with your life and your death. Then you, too, will be a Silhouette, a woman behind the greatest Man of all time, Jesus.